S0-AFE-490

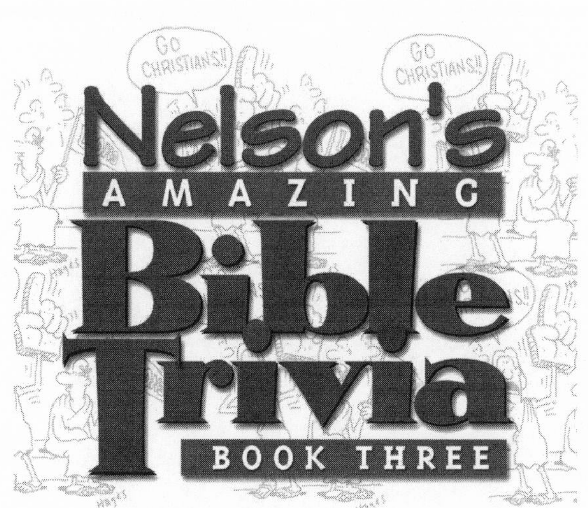
GO CHRISTIANS!!
GO CHRISTIANS!!
Nelson's
AMAZING
Bible
Trivia
BOOK THREE
Hayes
Hayes

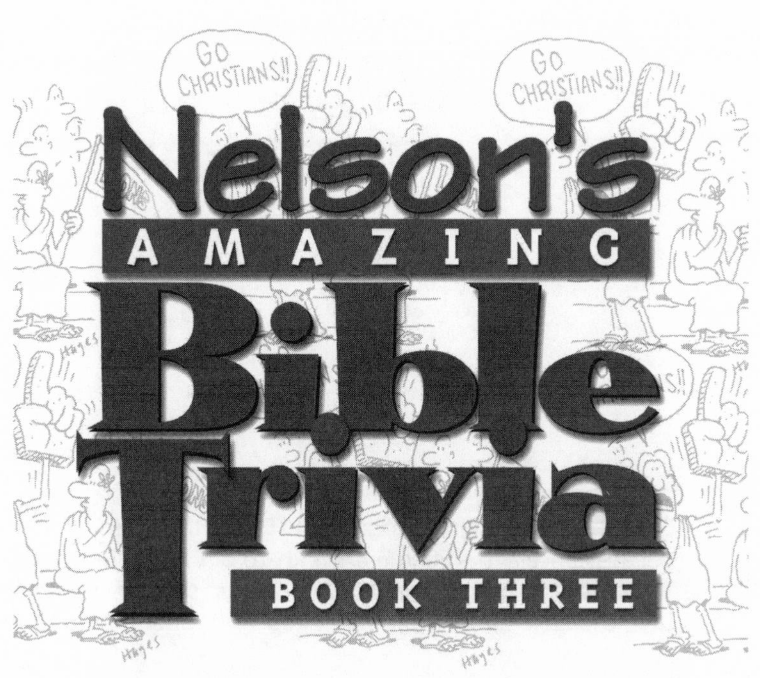

Nelson's Amazing Bible Trivia Book Three

Lowell D. Streiker

THOMAS NELSON PUBLISHERS
Nashville

Special thanks to Agnes Stogdell and Elizabeth Jensen for their editorial assistance and to Carrie L. Clickhard of CL Enterprises and Word Works for her encouragement and artistic support. Carrie contributed the Bible math puzzles that appear throughout this book.

Printed in Nashville, Tennessee, by Thomas Nelson, Inc.

ISBN 0-7852-4593-6

Printed in the United States of America

1 2 3 4 5 — 05 04 03 02 01

Table of Contents

Foreword

> Half the books of the Bible can be read in ten to forty-five minutes each, and many of them can be read in less than twenty. The entire Old and New Testaments can be read aloud slowly and with expression in less than seventy-one hours.
>
> —Wilbur M. Smith

When I became a Christian at a youth rally many years ago, I wanted to know what the Bible said. That meant reading the Bible from front to back, discussing the Bible with learned individuals, reading numerous books about the Bible such as commentaries, histories, archaeological records, etc., studying Hebrew and Greek—the languages in which the Scriptures were originally written. In other words, I became a voracious collector of *information about the Bible.*

As I matured, my focus gradually changed from gathering data to applying the teachings of the Scriptures to my own life. That has turned out to be a lifelong occupation!

Like a good journalist, as a Bible scholar you will always want to get your facts right. Well, consider the Bible your journalism assignment and see how much you know about its what, who, why, where, when, and how. In this book, you will find the widest variety of quizzes and puzzles ever assembled into a single Bible trivia book. Included are the following:

- Multiple Choice Quizzes
- Fill-in-the-Blank Quizzes
- Bible Math Exercises
- True or False Quizzes
- Crossword Puzzles
- Short Answer Quizzes
- Word Scramble Exercises
- Bible Jeopardy (I give you the answers and you must come up with the questions.)
- Matching Questions with Answers
- Word Find Exercises
- Enigma (You solve the mystery.)
- Crazy Quotations
- Bible Character Quizzes
- Quotefalls
- Bible Crisscross Exercises

This volume is a travel guide to the contents of the Bible. By yourself or with your friends, travel through the what, who, why, when, where, and how of the Bible by taking the tests, solving the puzzles, and finding pleasure in the fact-filled and humorous asides. In the end, you will know a great deal more about the Bible than you did when you started the journey.

At the same time, I trust you will discover that the Bible is more than names, places, battles, miracles, parables, prophecies, maxims, and prayers. As the author of the Book of Hebrews declares: "the word of God is living and powerful, and sharper than any two-edged sword, . . .

and is a discerner of the thoughts and intents of the heart'' (Heb. 4:12). No matter how much one knows about the Bible, it is important to keep in mind that *other books were given for our information; the Bible was given for our transformation.* May you find both information and transformation throughout this book.

—Lowell D. Streiker

Preface

A vast majority of Americans believe the Bible is the Word of God. Yet the contents of the Bible remain generally unknown. David F. Nygren observes, *"If all the neglected Bibles were dusted simultaneously, we would have a record dust storm, and the sun would go into eclipse for a whole week!"*

We have many excuses for ignoring the Bible, the chief one being that it is too hard to comprehend. But as Mark Twain once observed, "Most people are bothered by those Scripture passages they cannot understand. The passages which trouble me most are those which I *do* understand."

Pollster George Gallup, Jr. calls America a "nation of biblical illiterates." Only four in 10 Americans know that Jesus delivered the Sermon on the Mount. A majority of our fellow citizens cannot name the four Gospels. Only three in 10 teenagers know why Easter is celebrated. Two-thirds of Americans believe there are few, if any, absolute principles to direct human behavior.

All of which leads former Secretary of Education William Bennett to conclude that, "We have become the kind of society that civilized countries used to send missionaries to."

Although we are a nation of churchgoers, we have lost the Bible-reading habit.

If Bible reading is no longer a practice among Americans, it is probably because the book appears so daunting to those unfamiliar with it. The copy I use runs 1,735 closely printed pages, and of course the Bible is not like a typical book with a consistent and a modest number of characters. Moreover, you can't just sneak a look at the end to discover how the story turns out.

I have always been grateful for the way the Gideons use the back pages of their Bibles to assist lonely travelers in finding their way to the answers they need. Dr. Lowell Streiker does much the same thing for all of us, and he does it with wit and a great sense of fun. Plenty of people expand their vocabularies by working crossword puzzles, and everyone learns from quizzes and games. What a wonderful idea to become conversant with the Bible in the same ways!

I invite you to learn about the Bible and have fun doing it! Revel in revelation!

David Yount

David Yount's syndicated column, "Amazing Grace," appears in newspapers with a combined readership of 25 million. Three of his recent books have been Book-of-the-Month Club bestsellers, and he hosts a daily cable television show. He serves as vice chairman of the Washington Theological Consortium.

Bible Journalism

MULTIPLE CHOICE

1. **Who was Simon Peter's brother?**
   A. James
   B. Andrew
   C. John
   D. Simple Simon

2. **For the miracle at the wedding in Cana, how many stone jars did Jesus tell the servants to fill with water?**
   A. five
   B. six
   C. seven
   D. seven times seventy-seven

ANSWERS
p. 30

3. **Sick people waited at the Pool of Bethesda for the angel to:**
   A. cure them
   B. dry up the water
   C. touch the water
   D. perform show tunes

4. **When Jesus told the weeping people that Jairus' daughter was not dead, they:**
   A. laughed at him
   B. continued crying
   C. went home
   D. did back flips

5. How many times did Jesus say we should forgive others?

A. seven
B. never, if they are unrepentant
C. always
D. only if they are sorry

6. Jesus said that when we pray we must:

A. ask twice
B. ask for things only once
C. never give up
D. pretend to be using a phone

7. **Lazarus died in what town?**
   A. Jerusalem
   B. Nazareth
   C. Bethany
   D. Funky town

8. **After His resurrection, how many disciples did Jesus talk to on the road to Emmaus?**
   A. Two
   B. Five
   C. Twelve
   D. All of them

ANSWERS p. 30

9. **Whom did the apostles choose to replace Judas?**
   A. Jude
   B. Joseph
   C. Matthias
   D. Alf

10. **When the blind man told the leaders that Jesus had cured him, they:**
   A. believed him
   B. said Jesus was not from God

Q. What else did Jesus say at the Last Supper?
A. "Everyone who wants to be in the picture, get on this side of the table."

C. wanted to know more
D. blinded him

Source: Cliff Leitch, www.twopaths.com, adapted.

FILL IN THE BLANKS

1. Because he was defeated in battle, King _________ committed suicide.

2. _______________________, the mighty man of valor, was afflicted with leprosy.

3. While still a boy, ______________ was once sent to carry to his brothers some loaves and some parched grain. The army to which his brothers belonged gained a great victory when the boy killed ____________.

4. ____________ was arrayed in scarlet and gold with a chain about his neck after surviving the lions' den.

5. The hands of __________________ were upheld by ____________ and ____________, which caused the armies of Israel to be victorious.

6. _________ entertained an angel unawares by offering a burnt offering in the flames where the angel ascended.

7. _________________ was successor to David, King of Israel.

8. Manoah was _____________ father.

9. ________________ was called from the plow to be a prophet for the Lord.

10. ________________ partook of a meal prepared by an angel, and he was sustained forty days and nights during his trek to Mount Horeb.

WORD BANK

Elijah	Saul	Solomon	
Daniel	Naaman	Manoah	
Elisha	Goliath	Samson's	
Aaron	David	Moses	Hur

ANSWERS p. 31

BIBLE MATH

At Thanksgiving we thank God for all the good things in our lives. Solve the puzzle below and learn why it is God we thank! Each answer is a number that matches a letter of the alphabet (A=1, B=2, C=3 . . .). Put that letter in the blanks and find the missing words. The first one is done for you.

1st Word

Pharaoh's plagues – 3 = 7 = G

Commandments + 5 = ___ = ___

Apostles + 3 = ___ = ___

Days Joshua circled Jericho – 3 = ___ = ___

2nd Word

Horsemen in Revelation + 3 = ___ = ___

Sons of Noah × 3 = ___ = ___

Peter's denials × 2 = ___ = ___

Commandments × 2 = ___ = ___

Jesus days in desert – 21 = ___ = ___

3rd Word

Beatitudes – 4 = ___ = ___

New Testament books – 9 = ___ = ___

Tribes of Israel + 3 = ___ = ___

Years Jacob worked for Rachel – 1 = ___ = ___

4th Word

Trinity – 2 = ___ = ___

People in Eden = ___ = ___

Friends of Job × 5 = ___ = ___

Days of Rain – 18 = ___ = ___

Snakes in Eden X 5 = ___ = ___

G ___ ___ ___   ___ ___ ___ ___ ___ come ___ ___ ___ ___

___ ___ ___ ___ ___.

TRUE OR FALSE?

ANSWERS p. 32

1. The miracle of Gideon's fleece (Judges 6:36–40) is the most remarkable event in the Bible that was announced by shepherds.

2. Faith, hope, charity, forbearance, and tolerance are five things to which we are commanded in the Bible to hold fast.

3. The Ark of the Covenant contained only the staff of Moses.

4. A gentle and quiet spirit is the most beautiful ornament of a Christian woman, according to 1 Peter 3:3–4.

5. "Jesus" is the one word in Scripture that is said to contain the whole law.

6. James compares the Word of God to a mirror.

7. Felix is an example of one stifling religious convictions.

8. Festus, the governor of Damascus, endeavored to take St. Paul and make him a prisoner.

9. The color of the sky in the morning is mentioned by Jesus as a sign of the coming rain.

10. Thirty pieces of silver was the value of the books burned at Ephesus by those who practiced magic.

CROSSWORD PUZZLE

ANSWERS p. 34

■	■	■	1	2	3		4	5	6	■	■	■
■	7					■	8				9	■
■		■	10			11				■		■
12		13	■	14					■	15		16
17			18	■	19			■	20			
21				22		■	23	24				
	■	25			■	■	■	26			■	
27	28				29	■	30				31	
32				■	33	34		■	35			
36			■	37				38	■	39		
■		■	40						41	■		■
■	42					■	43					■
■	■	■	44							■	■	■

Across

1. Paul was his mentor.
7. A lyric poem in which a long verse is followed by a shorter one.
8. What Moses was hidden by.
10. They lived on the west coast of Asia Minor.
12. I.
14. Old kind of lace, or what you would call Mr. and Mrs. Lacy.
15. Classified ____________.
17. Saul's household servant.
19. Abbrev. for cylinder.
20. Society for the Teaching of the Old Testament.
21. To make possible.
23. Famous for her dance that made John lose his head.
25. 24 hours.
26. Nickname of Paul's best friend.
27. Made iridescent.
30. Basic hard labor.
32. Father of Rizpah.
33. My friend (in French).
35. He stood at the pulpit and read the Law.
36. Norse myths.
37. So (old form).
39. Forever.
40. Inhabitant of Zair in Edom.
42. Ill will.

43. Moses' mouthpiece.
44. The Lotus (Also "A.B. MULEN" spelled backwards).

Down

1. Grateful king who brought David silver and gold.
2. Forbidden statues.
3. Ketcham's Dennis.
4. Places to ride horses.
5. Egg-makers.
6. Indeed!
7. A brand of pocket watches.
9. There was a hot time in this old town one night.
11. Brrr!
12. Hezekiah.
13. Prophet: Only had time to say a few words.
15. To break down in a tiny form.
16. Star quality.
18. To disconcert or embarrass.
20. Astral; or add a "p" and you have the ropelike substance that holds a screen in place.
22. Caustic substance.
24. Homonym of a number more than seven.
28. Crowds out of control.
29. If he lived today, he would have become a circus performer with his own wild cat act.
30. A real soul singer on the other shore.

31. Pertaining to the god of war.

34. To injure and subtract from an object's beauty.

37. Enter through the narrow one.

38. To injure with a sharp object.

40. A desert in eastern Arabia.

41. A long time.

SHORT ANSWER

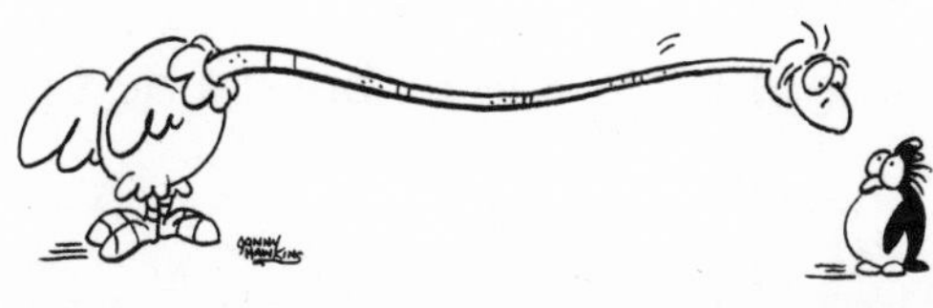

1. Who did Paul exhort to be "a worker who does not need to be ashamed"? ____________________

2. With what words did Christ declare his perfection?

____

3. What two things did Paul say are necessary for salvation? ____________________

4. What is Paul's great verse regarding the inspiration of the Scriptures? ____________________

5. On what occasion did Christ say, "Foxes have holes and the birds of the air have nests, but the Son of man has nowhere to lay his head"? ____________________

____

6. Who described the devil as a murderer from the beginning? What was the rest of his description?

____

7. How did Christ state his pre-existence? __________

____

8. Who said, "If the Son makes you free, you shall be free indeed."? To whom did he say it? __________

____

9. In what connection did Christ say, "The night comes, when no man can work"? __________

____

10. What is Paul's advice about anger? __________

____

WORD SCRAMBLE

1. Who fed Elijah in the desert? EVRAN _ _ _ _ _

2. Who swallowed Jonah? EWLAH _ _ _ _ _

3. Who carried Jesus into Jerusalem? YKDENO _ _ _ _ _ _

4. Who helped Noah find land? VEOD _ _ _ _

5. Who plagued Pharaoh? GFORS _ _ _ _ _

HOW ABOUT THAT!

The word "Bible" is nowhere found in the Bible. The word is taken from the Greek word "biblia" which means "books" and refers to those books acknowledged by Christians as part of the canon of inspired scriptures.

6. Who was breakfast for John the Baptist? CSTULOS _ _ _ _ _ _ _

7. Who bit the Israelites in the desert? SPA _ _ _

8. Who took Isaac's place? EPEHS _ _ _ _ _

9. Who ignored Daniel? SNOLI _ _ _ _ _

10. Who tempted Adam and Eve? KESAN _ _ _ _ _

ANSWERS p. 36

BIBLE JEOPARDY

$100
$200
$300
$400
DAILY DOUBLE
$500
$600
$700
$800
$900

Here are the answers. Do you know the questions?

1. This place is where the disciples were first called Christians.
2. This European city first heard Christian preaching.
3. Christ's first miracle was performed here.
4. This was Christ's home for the first thirty years of his life.
5. This was the rendezvous point of the Israelites as they were leaving Egypt.
6. This was where Jesus was betrayed with a kiss.
7. The first Christian missionaries did their work here.
8. The first missionary sermon (of which we have an extended report) was preached here.

MATCHING

1. "Why are you angry? And why has your countenance fallen?"	a. The Lord

2. "What is this you have done to me? Why did you not tell me that she was your wife?"

3. "Why did Sarah laugh, saying, 'Shall I surely bear a child, since I am old?' "

4. "Why do you look at once another?"

5. "Why do you cry to me? Tell the children of Israel to go forward."

6. "Why have you struck your donkey these three times?"

7. "O my lord, if the Lord is with us, why then has all this happened to us?"

8. "Why have you disturbed me by bringing me up?"

9. "Why have you despised the commandment of the Lord, to do evil in his sight?"

10. Why is your spirit so sullen that you eat no food?

11. "Why have you done this?"

12. "Why have you not repaired the damages of the temple?"

b. The angel of the Lord

c. Samuel

d. Nathan

e. Mariners

f. Pharaoh

g. King Jehoash

h. Jacob

i. Jezebel

j. Gideon

WORD FIND

Find the many names of Jesus in the puzzle. The letters left over spell the puzzle's answer.

```
M E S S I A H A
S U S E J A H D
A S L A G P K R
V V A E L I E O
I M M A N U E L
O O B G D R O W
R E D E E M E R
U S C H R I S T
```

Alpha	Christ
Immanuel	King
Jesus	Lord
Lamb	Omega
Messiah	Savior
Redeemer	Word

Jesus came to earth to _ _ _ _   _ _!

ENIGMA

ANSWERS p. 38

Faith shall be swallowed up in sight,
Hope in fulfillment end,
When on our twilight life the light
Of heaven shall descend.

A sister-grace to these, more great,
Shall brighten when they wane;
O let us more and more to this,
Even in this life attain!

The first letters of the following answers will give the name of this most excellent grace:

1. The grandmother of Timothy.
2. The good servant of a wicked king, who kept one hundred prophets of the Lord from the vengeance of the queen.
3. A queen who resisted her husband's command and was deposed.
4. A good man, but a bad father.

QUOTEFALL

ANSWERS p. 39

Solve the puzzle by moving the letters to form words. The letters can only be moved to another place in the same column. Black boxes indicate the spaces between words. Each word begins in the left side of the box.

	N			L	E	R	S			F		T		E
	S	D	O	R	D	O	Y		I	H		I	H	H
A	V	I	R	V	H	R	C	O	T	S	A	T	H	H
A	W	O	C	T	O	I	U	R	M	E	A	T	T	E
			■					■			■			
■								■					■	
		■									■			
■									■					

BIBLE CRISSCROSS

These are the names of Biblical locations. Each name begins with the last letter of the preceding word.

1. Where Jesus performed His first miracle. ___ ___ ___ ___
2. Where the disciples were first called Christians. ___ ___ ___ ___ ___ ___ ___
3. Where Moses saw the burning bush. ___ ___ ___ ___ ___
4. Where Jesus was born. ___ ___ ___ ___ ___ ___ ___ ___ ___
5. The Great Sea. ___ ___ ___ ___ ___ ___ ___ ___ ___ ___ ___ ___ ___
6. Where Jesus lived as a boy. ___ ___ ___ ___ ___ ___ ___ ___
7. Home of Abraham after he left Lot. ___ ___ ___ ___ ___ ___
8. River of Egypt. ___ ___ ___ ___
9. The country Joseph saved from famine. ___ ___ ___ ___ ___

ANSWERS p. 39

10. A Phoenician commercial city. ___ ___ ___ ___
11. River of Babylon. ___ ___ ___ ___ ___ ___ ___ ___ ___ ___
12. Where Moses received the Ten Commandments. ___ ___ ___ ___ ___

13. Eastern boundary of the Persian Empire.

__ __ __ __ __

14. Where Noah's ark landed. __ __ __ __ __ __

15. Where Jonah was trying to go.

__ __ __ __ __ __ __ __ __

16. Mountain of the Lebanon range. __ __ __ __ __ __

17. A land to the east of Eden. __ __ __

18. An ancient city famous for its steel.

__ __ __ __ __ __ __ __

19. The land of the Good Samaritan.

__ __ __ __ __ __ __ __

ANSWERS
p. 40

20. Capital of Greece. __ __ __ __ __ __

21. City destroyed with Gomorrah. __ __ __ __ __

22. "Come over to __ __ __ __ __ __ __ __ __ and help us."

23. City taken by Joshua. __ __

John Whitehall, a wealthy Texan, wanted to send his mother an unusual, expensive gift for Mother's Day. The owner of a pet shop told him of a mynah bird worth well over twenty thousand dollars. "What makes this bird so valuable?" asked Whitehall. The owner responded, "This mynah bird is the only one in the world that can recite the Lord's Prayer, the twenty-third Psalm, and 1 Corinthians 13."

"I'll take it," said the Texan. "I don't care how much it costs. Mother is worth it, and she'll get so much comfort hearing it recite Scripture." He wrote a check and had it shipped off to his mother.

The Monday after Mother's Day he called her long distance. "Did you get my present?"

"I certainly did, and thank you."

"And how did you like the bird?"

"Oh son, it was delicious!"

24. City of Lycaonia where Paul was persecuted.

__ __ __ __ __ __ __

25. The mountain on which Solomon's temple was built. __ __ __ __ __ __ __

SHORT ANSWER

1. Who built the first city? ____________________

2. Who was the first sacred historian? ____________________

3. Who was the first judge? ____________________

4. Who was the first pilgrim? ____________________

5. Who was the first shepherd mentioned in the Scriptures? ____________________

6. Who told the first lie as recorded in the Scriptures?

____

7. Who was the first Jewish high priest? ____________________

8. Who was the first woman? ____________________

9. Who was the first gardener? ____________________

10. Who first wore the bridal veil? ____________________

TRUE OR FALSE?

The Bible says:

1. Joseph went from Nazareth to Bethlehem.
2. When Joseph and Mary traveled to Bethlehem, Mary rode a donkey, but Joseph walked.
3. The innkeeper told Joseph there was no room in the inn.

HOW ABOUT THAT!

The first translation of the English Bible was initiated by John Wycliffe and completed by John Purvey in 1388.

4. Jesus was born on the same night Joseph and Mary arrived in Bethlehem.
5. Mary gave birth to her first-born son, wrapped him in swaddling cloths and laid Him in a manger.
6. Straw filled the manger where Jesus was.
7. Jesus was born on a cold winter's night.

8. Sheep stood next to the manger.

9. The stable was built of wood.

10. Joseph and Mary named Jesus the night He was born.

11. Some of the animals woke the baby Jesus, but He didn't cry.

12. The shepherds were terrified when an angel of the Lord appeared to them, announcing Christ's birth.

13. The shepherds, then the Magi/wisemen, came to the manger.

14. The shepherds and the Magi saw His star.

ANSWERS p. 41

15. The Magi were from the East.

16. King Herod sent the Magi to Bethlehem.

17. The Magi arrived on camels.

18. Three Magi visited Bethlehem.

19. The Magi came to a house where the child and His mother were.

Q. What is the difference between opium and Abraham?

A. One is the juice of the poppy, and the other is the poppy of the Jews.

20. After having found the child, the Magi were warned not to go back to Herod.

Source: Concept and design by Karen Geffert in collaboration with Jean Kincaid, Ph.D. and John E. Wootton, Ph.D. © 1995–2000 by the Virtual Church (http://www.virtualchurch.org). Adapted by LDS.

MULTIPLE CHOICE

1. **What did Jesus say were the two great commandments?**
   A. "Honor your father and mother" and "Keep the Sabbath"
   B. "Do to others what you would have them do to you" and "walk the extra mile"
   C. "You shall love the Lord your God with all your heart, with all your soul, with all your mind, and with all your strength" and "You shall love your neighbor as yourself"
   D. "Go and sin no more" and "Repent! The kingdom of God is at hand"
   E. "Wash yourself daily" and "Have your pet spayed or neutered"

2. **What does Holy Week in the church commemorate?**
   A. The birth of Jesus
   B. The ascension of Jesus
   C. The giving of the Holy Spirit
   D. The last week of Jesus' earthly life

E. The period between Christmas and Ground Hog's Day

3. What happened on Palm Sunday?

A. Jesus was born in the City of Palms
B. Judas chopped down his palm tree
C. The triumphal entry into Jerusalem
D. The arrest of Jesus
E. The high-five was invented

HOW ABOUT THAT!

In the New International Version of the Bible the shortest verse is not "Jesus wept" (John 11:35), but "He said" (Job 3:2).

4. What did the people shout when Jesus entered Jerusalem?

A. "Crucify him!"
B. "Hosanna!"
C. "We know who our father is"
D. "The LORD is my shepherd"
E. "Geronimo!"

5. What feast was being celebrated?

A. The Festival of Lights
B. The Day of Atonement

C. None; It was a fast week
D. Passover
E. The Feast of Undercooked Pork Products

6. **What does the Passover commemorate?**
   A. Crossing the River Jordan
   B. Climbing Mount Sinai
   C. David's victory over Goliath
   D. The Exodus
   E. The first Olympic games

7. **At present, Passover occurs close to what Christian holy day?**
   A. Christmas
   B. Pentecost
   C. Easter
   D. None of the above
   E. All Hallows' Eve

ANSWERS p. 44

8. **What did Jesus do on Monday of Holy Week?**
   A. Drove money changers out of the temple
   B. Washed his disciples feet
   C. Visited Mary and Martha
   D. Allowed little children to come to him
   E. Watched Monday Night Football

9. **What was the Last Supper?**
   A. The meal that Lazarus ate before he died
   B. Stephen's dinner
   C. Joshua's final meal in the wilderness
   D. Jesus and the twelve ate the Passover together (their last meal with him)
   E. Two cans of corn and an old fish

10. What service in church commemorates the Last Supper?

A. Maundy Thursday
B. Christmas breakfast
C. Communion; also known as the Lord's Supper or the Eucharist
D. Baptism
E. The pot-luck dinner

ANSWERS TO: BIBLE JOURNALISM

MULTIPLE CHOICE

#	ANSWER	REFERENCE
1.	b.	Matthew 4:18
2.	b.	John 2:6–7
3.	c.	John 5:2–4
4.	a.	Mark 5:39–40
5.	c.	Matthew 18:22
6.	c.	Luke 11:5–13, 18:1–8
7.	c.	John 11:1–14
8.	a.	Luke 24:13–18
9.	c.	Acts 1:15–26
10.	b.	John 9:1–16

FILL IN THE BLANKS

#	ANSWER	REFERENCE
1.	Saul	1 Chronicles 10:4
2.	Naaman	2 Kings 5:1
3.	David, Goliath	1 Samuel 17:12, 24
4.	Daniel	Daniel 5:7, 16, 29

#	ANSWER	REFERENCE
5.	Moses, Aaron, Hur	Exodus 17:9, 13
6.	Manoah	Judges 13:20
7.	Solomon	1 Kings 5:1
8.	Samson's	Judges 13:21
9.	Elisha	1 Kings 19:20
10.	Elijah	1 Kings 19:8, 9

BIBLE MATH

#	ANSWER		
1.	Pharaoh's plagues – 3	= 7	= G
	Commandments + 5	= 15	= O
	Apostles + 3	= 15	= O
	Days Joshua circled Jericho – 3	= 4	= D
2.	Horsemen in Revelation + 3	= 7	= G
	Sons of Noah × 3	= 9	= I
	Peter's denials × 2	= 6	= F
	Commandments × 2	= 20	= T
	Jesus days in desert – 21	= 19	= S

BIBLE MATH—cont'd

#	ANSWER		
3.	Beatitudes – 4	= 6	= F
	New Testament books – 9	= 18	= R
	Tribes of Israel + 3	= 15	= O
	Years Jacob worked for Rachel – 1	= 14	= M
4.	Trinity – 2	= 1	= A
	People in Eden	= 2	= B
	Friends of Job × 5	= 15	= O
	Days of Rain – 18	= 22	= V
	Snakes in Eden × 5	= 5	= E

G O O D G I F T S come F R O M A B O V E.

TRUE OR FALSE

#	ANSWER	REFERENCE
1.	False; The birth of Christ	Luke 2:8
2.	False.	
	a. That which is good	1 Thessalonians 5:21
	b. The pattern of sound words	2 Timothy 1:13

#	ANSWER	REFERENCE
	c. Our confidence	Hebrews 3:14
	d. Our confession	Hebrews 4:14
	e. That which you have already	Revelation 2:25
3.	False; According to Hebrews 9:4, "the golden censer and the ark of the covenant overlaid on all sides with gold, in which were the golden pot that had the manna, Aaron's rod that budded, and the tablets of the covenant."	Hebrews 9:4
4.	True.	1 Peter 3:4
5.	False; Love	Romans 13:10
6.	True.	James 1:23
7.	True.	Acts 24:25
8.	False; The governor is not named.	2 Corinthians 11:32
9.	True.	Matthew 16:2
10.	False; Fifty thousand pieces of silver.	Acts 19:19

CROSSWORD PUZZLE

■	■	■	1 T	2 I	3 M	O	4 T	5 H	6 Y	■	■	■
■	7 E	P	O	D	E	■	8 R	E	E	D	9 S	■
■	L	■	10 I	O	N	11 I	A	N	S	■	O	■
12 E	G	13 O	■	14 L	A	C	I	S	■	15 A	D	16 S
17 Z	I	B	18 A	■	19 C	Y	L	■	20 S	T	O	T
21 E	N	A	B	22 L	E	■	23 S	24 A	L	O	M	E
K	■	25 D	A	Y	■	■	■	26 T	I	M	■	L
27 I	28 R	I	S	E	29 D	■	30 M	E	N	I	31 A	L
32 A	I	A	E	■	33 A	34 M	I	■	35 E	Z	R	A
36 S	O	H	■	37 G	N	A	R	38 S	■	39 E	E	R
■	T	■	40 Z	A	I	R	I	T	41 E	■	A	■
■	42 S	P	I	T	E	■	43 A	A	R	O	N	■
■	■	■	44 N	E	L	U	M	B	A	■	■	■

SHORT ANSWER

# ANSWER	REFERENCE
1. Timothy.	2 Timothy 2:15
2. "I do always those things that please Him" (the Father).	John 8:29

#	ANSWER	REFERENCE
3.	To confess the Lord Jesus and to believe in his resurrection.	Romans 10:9
4.	"All Scripture is given by inspiration of God, and is profitable for doctrine, for reproof, for correction, for instruction in righteousness."	2 Timothy 3:16
5.	When a scribe said that he would follow Christ wherever he went.	Matthew 8:19, 20
6.	Christ, who added, "He is a liar, and the father of it."	John 8:44
7.	"Before Abraham was, I am."	John 8:58
8.	Christ said it to believing Jews who had been boasting of their freedom from bondage.	John 8:32
9.	Just before opening the eyes of the man born blind.	John 9:4
10.	"Be angry, and do not sin; do not let the sun go down on your wrath."	Ephesians 4:26

WORD SCRAMBLE

#	ANSWER
1.	Raven
2.	Whale
3.	Donkey
4.	Dove
5.	Frogs
6.	Locusts
7.	Asp
8.	Sheep
9.	Lions
10.	Snake

BIBLE JEOPARDY

#	ANSWER	REFERENCE
1.	Where is Antioch?	Acts 11:26
2.	Where is Philippi?	Acts 16:12–13
3.	Where is Cana of Galilee?	John 2:1—11:3
4.	Where is Nazareth in Galilee?	Luke 2:39–51
5.	Where is Succoth?	Exodus 12:37
6.	Where is the Garden of Gethsemane?	Matthew 26:36–56; John 18:1–12

#	ANSWER	REFERENCE
7.	Where is the island of Cyprus? *and* Where is the city of Salamis?	Acts 13
8.	Where is Antioch in Pisidia?	Acts 13:14–42

MATCHING

#		ANSWER	REFERENCE
1.	a.	The Lord (to Cain)	Genesis 4:6
2.	f.	Pharaoh (to Abram)	Genesis 12:18–19
3.	a.	The Lord (to Abraham)	Genesis 18:13
4.	h.	Jacob (to his sons)	Genesis 42:1
5.	a.	The Lord (to Moses)	Exodus 14:15
6.	b.	The Angel of the Lord (to Balaam)	Numbers 22:32
7.	j.	Gideon (to the Angel of the Lord)	Judges 6:13
8.	c.	Samuel (to Saul)	1 Samuel 28:15
9.	d.	Nathan (to David)	2 Samuel 12:9
10.	i.	Jezebel (to Ahab)	1 Kings 21:5
11.	e.	The Mariners (to Jonah)	Jonah 1:10
12.	g.	King Jehoash (to Jehoiada the priest)	2 Kings 12:7

WORD FIND

After finding the many names of Jesus in the puzzle, the letters left over spell the puzzle's answer.

```
M E S S I A H A
S U S E J A H D
A S L A G P K R
V V A E L I E O
I M M A N U E L
O O B G D R O W
R E D E E M E R
U S C H R I S T
```

Alpha	Christ
Immanuel	King
Jesus	Lord
Lamb	Omega
Messiah	Savior
Redeemer	Word

Jesus came to earth to S A V E U S!

ENIGMA

# ANSWER	REFERENCE
"LOVE."	
1. **L**-ois	2 Timothy 1:5
2. **O**-badiah	1 Kings 18:4
3. **V**-ashti	Esther 1:10–19
4. **E**-li	1 Samuel 3:13

1 Corinthians 13:13: "And now abide faith, hope, love, these three; but the greatest of these is love."

1 John 4:11: "Beloved, if God so loved us, we also ought to love one another."

QUOTEFALL

	N			L	E	R	S			F		T		E
	S	D	O	R	D	O	Y		I	H		I	H	H
A	V	I	R	V	H	R	C	O	T	S	A	T	H	H
A	W	O	C	T	O	I	U	R	M	E	A	T	T	E
A	N	D	■	T	H	I	S	■	I	S	■	T	H	E
■	V	I	C	T	O	R	Y	■	T	H	A	T	■	H
A	S	■	O	V	E	R	C	O	M	E	■	T	H	E
■	W	O	R	L	D	O	U	R	■	F	A	I	T	H

BIBLE CRISSCROSS

 # ANSWER

1. Cana
2. Antioch
3. Horeb
4. Bethlehem
5. Mediterranean
6. Nazareth
7. Hebron
8. Nile
9. Egypt
10. Tyre
11. Euphrates

BIBLE CRISSCROSS—cont'd

#	ANSWER
12.	Sinai
13.	India
14.	Ararat
15.	Tarshish
16.	Hermon
17.	Nod
18.	Damascus
19.	Samaria
20.	Athens
21.	Sodom
22.	Macedonia
23.	Ai
24.	Iconium
25.	Moriah

SHORT ANSWER

#	ANSWER	REFERENCE
1.	Cain	Genesis 4:17
2.	Moses	Numbers 1:1
3.	Moses	Exodus 18:13

#	ANSWER	REFERENCE
4.	Abram	Genesis 12:1, 6
5.	Abel	Genesis 4:4
6.	Cain	Genesis 4:8
7.	Aaron	Exodus 28:1
8.	Eve	Genesis 2:23
9.	Adam	Genesis 2:15
10.	Rebekah	Genesis 24:64, 65

TRUE OR FALSE

#	ANSWER	REFERENCE
1.	True.	Luke 2:4
2.	False; Although it's possible Mary rode a donkey because of her condition, this is not stated in the Scriptures.	
3.	False; Many Christmas pageants include a scene where Joseph has a door slammed rudely in his face. However, an innkeeper isn't actually mentioned in Scripture.	Luke 2:7

TRUE OR FALSE—cont'd

#	ANSWER	REFERENCE
4.	False; We do not know exactly when Jesus was born.	Luke 2:6
5.	True.	Luke 2:7
6.	False; The Scriptures don't specify straw.	
7.	False; You'll find this in the opening stanza of "The First Noel," not Scripture.	
8.	False; No nativity set seems complete without a few sheep facing the manger. But the biblical account mentions only flocks in nearby fields.	Luke 2:8
9.	False; No stable is mentioned in either Matthew or Luke.	
10.	False; He was given the name by an angel before conception and it was publicly confirmed at his circumcision.	Luke 1:31; 2:21
11.	False; This is found in Martin Luther's "Away in a Manger," not Scripture.	

#	ANSWER	REFERENCE
12.	True.	Luke 2:9.13
13.	False; Nativity scenes have several Magi at the manger, but your Bible will not have them present.	Matthew 2:11; Luke 2:16
14.	False. Although we're told the Magi saw the star we have no scriptural evidence the shepherds did.	Matthew 2:2–10
15.	True.	Matthew 2:1
16.	True.	Matthew 2:8
17.	False; Although it's likely they used camels for transportation, you won't find them mentioned in the account.	
18.	False; When you sing "The First Noel" or "We Three Kings," remember we are not told how many Magi traveled to Bethlehem.	Matthew 2:11
19.	True.	Matthew 2:11
20.	True.	Matthew 2:12

MULTIPLE CHOICE

# ANSWER	REFERENCE
1. c.	Mark 12:29–31
2. d.	
3. c.	Matthew 21
4. b.	Matthew 21:9
5. d.	John 11:55
6. d.	Exodus 12
7. c.	
8. a.	Matthew 21:12; Mark 11:15
9. d.	Matthew 26:17–30
10. c.	

Who?

MULTIPLE CHOICE

1. **Jesus performed many miracles during His ministry, and they served as signs that the Kingdom of God had truly come. What was Jesus' first miracle?**
   A. Walking on water
   B. Turning water into wine
   C. Feeding 5,000 with the loaves and fishes
   D. Cursing the fig tree
   E. The turning of bread into toast

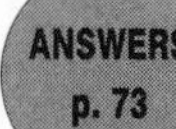
ANSWERS
p. 73

2. **Whose mother-in-law did Jesus heal when she had a fever?**
   A. Martha's
   B. Mary Magdalene's
   C. Matthew's
   D. Simon Peter's
   E. St. Nicholas'

3. **As Jesus and His disciples were crossing the Sea of Galilee in a boat, a terrible storm arose and threatened to drown them. Jesus rebuked the wind and waves and the storm disappeared. What was Jesus doing when the storm arose?**
   A. Praying
   B. Sleeping
   C. Eating a meal
   D. Explaining the parables to His disciples
   E. Watching *Survivor*

4. **Whose daughter did Jesus bring back to life?**
   A. Jairus'
   B. Herod's
   C. Paul Simon's
   D. Simon Peter's
   E. Martha's

5. **Jesus miraculously broke just a few loaves of bread and fishes and fed 5000 men, plus women and children. How many loaves and fishes did he start with?**
   A. 3 loaves and 2 fish
   B. 2 loaves and 3 fish
   C. 3 cloves and 2 dishes
   D. 5 loaves and 2 fish
   E. 2 loaves and 5 fish

6. **Which disciple walked on the water with Jesus?**
   A. James
   B. Matthew
   C. Peter
   D. Solomon
   E. Thomas

7. **Which disciples were with Jesus at His transfiguration, when "His face shone like the sun, and his clothes became as white as the light"?**
   A. Andrew, James, and Matthew
   B. Peter, James, and John
   C. Paul, Timothy, and Titus
   D. Thomas, Peter, and John
   E. Peter, Paul, and Mary

8. **When Jesus healed the man who was blind from birth, He made mud with His spit and put it on the man's eyes. What did He tell the man to do then?**
   A. Go pray in the synagogue.
   B. Go show himself to the Pharisees.
   C. See a physician.
   D. Wash his clothes in the tide.
   E. Wash in the pool of Siloam.

9. **What man did Jesus raise from the dead, after he had been dead four days?**
   A. John the Baptist
   B. Lazarus
   C. The Prodigal Son
   D. Elijah
   E. Moses

10. **What was Bartimaeus' affliction that Jesus healed?**
   A. Mad Cow Disease
   B. Lameness
   C. Viral Pneumonia
   D. Deafness
   E. Blindness

Cliff Leitch (TwoPath.com).

FILL IN THE BLANKS

1. ______________________ offered his own new tomb for the burial of Jesus.

2. The women did not go to the tomb of Jesus on the Sabbath because ____________ ____________ forbade it.

3. ________ ______________ kept watch at the tomb.

4. The three women brought ____________ to anoint the body of Jesus.

5. ____________ ____________ was the first to see the risen Jesus.

ANSWERS p. 74

6. The angel said, "He is ____________."

7. ____________ and ____________, two of his disciples ran to the sepulcher.

8. Thomas doubted the resurrection until he could ______________________________________.

9. The last command of Jesus was: "Go therefore and ________ ______________ of all the nations, baptizing them in the name of the Father and of the Son and of the Holy Spirit, teaching them to observe all things that I have commanded you."

10. The last promise of Jesus was, "Lo! I am ________ ____________________________."

WORD BANK

with you always, even unto the end of the age

Joseph of Arimathea   spices   Peter

Roman soldiers   John   risen   make disciples

Jewish law   Mary Magdalene

feel the nail prints with his own hands

BIBLE MATH

In Luke 18, the tax collector taught us an important lesson. Help the tax collector solve his math problems. Each answer is a number that matches a letter of the alphabet (A=1, B=2, C=3 . . .). Put that letter in the blanks and find the missing words. The first one is done for you.

1st Word

Seals in Revelation + 1 = 8 = H

New Testament books – 6 = ___ = ___

Tribes of Israel + 1 = ___ = ___

Snakes in Eden × 2 = ___ = ___

Peter's denials × 4 = ___ = ___

Commandments ÷ 2 = ___ = ___

Years in wilderness – 21 = ___ = ___

2nd Word

Number of Gospels + 1 = ___ = ___

Apostles X 2 = ___ = ___

Jesus' days in the tomb – 2 = ___ = ___

The commandments + 2 = ___ = ___

Noah's days of rain ÷ 2 = ___ = ___

Days of creation – 2 = ___ = ___

Trinity + 1 = ___ = ___

He who H ___ ___ ___ ___ ___ ___ himself will be

will be ___ ___ ___ ___ ___ ___ ___!

TRUE OR FALSE?

1. It was to James and John that Jesus said, "Come with me and I will make you fishers of men."

2. Jesus used five loaves and two fish to feed the five thousand.

Q. Who ran the first canning factory?

A. Noah. He had a boatful of preserved pairs.

3. Jesus taught the Lord's Prayer to his disciples.

4. Jesus often taught his message in stories known as allegories.

5. Parables are stories with a moral; "earthly stories with a heavenly meaning."

6. The best known parables include "the good son" and "the unjust virgins."

7. The Pharisees were Roman tax collectors.

8. Miracles of Jesus include walking on water and raising Jairus' daughter.

9. "Lord, save me" is the shortest verse in the Bible.

10. Jesus wept at the tomb of his friend Lazarus.

CROSSWORD PUZZLE

ANSWERS p. 77

1 2 3 4 5 6 7 8 9 10 11 12 13 14 15 16 17 18 19

Across

2. What event followed Jesus' baptism?
5. Who told the shepherds of Jesus' birth?
7. In what river was he baptized?
9. What event in the king's career brought the Holy Family back?
11. Where did the Holy Family go to escape the king?
12. Another name for the wise men.
13. Who baptized Jesus?
14. In what town did Mary and Joseph live?
16. Who first heard the news of Jesus' birth?
17. What precious metal did the wise men bring?
18. Where did Jesus go after his discussions in the temple?
19. John said: "I am not worthy to unlace his ______."

Down

1. What led the wise men?
3. About how old was he when he began to preach?
4. Who tried to kill the baby Jesus?
6. What brought Jesus' parents to Bethlehem?
8. What was Jesus' occupation?
10. Where was he born?
12. Who was Jesus' mother?
13. Who was Jesus' earthly father?
15. How old was he when he first discussed religion with the teachers at the temple?

SHORT ANSWER

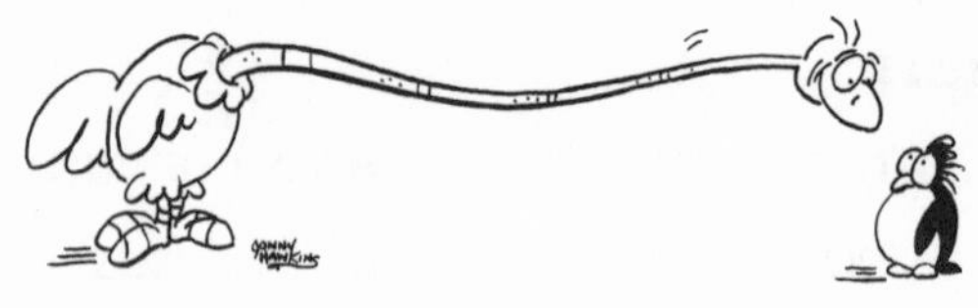

1. Who does the Bible describe as highway robbers?

____

2. Which King's life was endangered by a stone from the hand of a woman? _______________

3. Whose life was lengthened fifteen years in answer to prayer? _______________

4. Who wished to "die the death of the righteous?"

____

5. Who are the only three persons mentioned in the Bible whose names begin with the letter V?

____

6. What King in besieging a city set an example to his people and said: "What you have seen me do, make haste and do as I have done?" _______________

7. Who was made King of Judah at seven years of age after having been hidden for six years? _______________

8. What King closed the temple of God? _______________

9. Of whom and by whom was it said, they had "written bitter things against him"? ____________

10. What High Priest stood between the living and the dead and averted a plague that had already slain 14,700? ____________

WORD SCRAMBLE

Put the letters in correct order to spell the names of people in the book of Genesis.

1. SAACI _ _ _ _ _
2. HRSAA _ _ _ _ _
3. OMSSE _ _ _ _ _
4. BAJCO _ _ _ _ _
5. HANO _ _ _ _
6. MAAD _ _ _ _
7. PEJHOS _ _ _ _ _ _
8. CLERHA _ _ _ _ _ _
9. MAHBAAR _ _ _ _ _ _ _
10. BAEL _ _ _ _
11. MAMIRI _ _ _ _ _ _

ANSWERS p. 78

BIBLE JEOPARDY

$100	$200	$300	$400	DAILY DOUBLE	$500	$600	$700	$800	$900

Here are the answers. Do you know the questions?

1. The disciples did this to Jesus when he was arrested and led away.
2. He washed his hands of blame for Jesus' death.
3. The people cried this out, telling Pilate what to do with Jesus.
4. This is the day of Jesus' death.
5. This is the place of Jesus' death.
6. He survived on the cross this long.
7. These ladies were at the foot of the cross.
8. Jesus commended his mother to this disciple.

ANSWERS p. 79

Q. Who was the most ambitious man in the Bible?

A. Jonah—even a whale couldn't keep him down.

9. Jesus died around this time.

10. Jesus was this age when he died.

MATCHING

The questions are in the first column. The answers are in the second—in scrambled order. Can you make the right connections? (Warning: One answer is used twice!)

1. Who were hewers of wood and drawers of water?	a. Achan
2. With what people was the first battle fought by the Israelites after leaving Egypt?	b. Amalekites
3. Who hid one hundred prophets in a cave?	c. Gibeonites
4. In the funeral possession of whom do we find the first mention of horsemen?	d. Jacob
5. Who prophesied that the Jews should eat their own children?	e. Jeremiah
6. Who did the LORD make a terror to himself and his friends because he smote the prophet Jeremiah?	f. Joash
7. Who prophesied that Judah should be carried captive into Babylon and where is it recorded?	g. Obadiah

8. Who organized a collection of funds to repair the house of the LORD?	h. Pashur
9. What woman said, "I am weary of my life."?	i. Rebekah
10. What criminal in his confession said, "I saw, I coveted, I took."?	

WORD FIND

Find each of the Matriarchs listed below in the puzzle. Some are in a straight line up and down, some left to right, some on an angle (and backwards, of course). Circle each letter of each word. The letters left over spell out the secret puzzle message.

M	O	E	T	H	A	E	L	B
H	V	I	M	O	A	N	E	A
E	R	G	O	M	E	R	S	T
A	Z	I	P	P	O	R	A	H
H	R	Y	E	A	E	A	B	S
A	A	B	R	B	L	C	I	H
N	E	G	E	A	S	H	G	E
N	S	K	A	I	M	E	A	B
A	A	N	G	R	❤	L	I	A
H	T	E	B	A	Z	I	L	E

Abigail	Rachel
Bathsheba	Hannah
Rebekah	Eve
Elizabeth	Leah
Zipporah	Naomi
Gomer	Hagar
Mary	

_ _ _ _ _ _ _ _   _ _ _   _

_ _ _ _ _ _ _ _ _ ❤

ENIGMA NO. 1

ANSWERS p. 81

1. What prophet did the Savior's birthplace tell,
   When He came down as man, with men to dwell?

2. A term employed in God's most holy Word
   Which does His truth and faithfulness record.

3. A striking monument of heavenly grace,
   Who saw his blessed Savior face to face?

4. The village where our risen Lord appeared,
   And thus, two sorrowing disciples cheered.

5. A holy seer who lived in David's days,
   And sang to God in sweetest songs of praise?

6. To whom did God an holy angel send,
   That He to Peter's message might attend?

7. What bird does on its wings its offspring bear,
   An emblem of our Heavenly Father's care?

8. Who on King David's fortunes did attend,
   And in his trials proved a constant friend?

9. The land from which arose the world's true light,
   When all around were sunk in deepest night.

10. What prophet's lips were touched with holy fire,
    And spoke great words that still our hope inspire?

11. What beauteous plant did shadow forth our Lord,
    And of His much-loved church a type afford?

12. A stone the prophet Samuel did raise,
    His God for deliverance great to praise.

13. The ancestor of one renowned for grace,
    From whom descended the whole Jewish race.

14. A seer who led his people once to show
    Pity and mercy to a fallen foe.

15. What glorious time did shadow forth that day
    When from this earth the curse shall pass away?

16. A prince, who by a pious king was sent,
    That he might lead his people to repent?

17. What mystic word, inscribed on palace wall,
    By unknown hand, foretold great Babel's fall?

The initials take in order due their place,
And then are read calm words of heavenly grace
The last best gift that our Redeemer gave
To those loved friends He came from heaven to save
Oh Lord, give ear unto our earnest prayer,
And grant that we this blessed gift may share.

ENIGMA NO. 2

ANSWERS p. 82

1. The fifth son of a patriarch's earliest wife.

2. A prophet, here sailing, risked his life.

3. "An Israelite indeed," as Christ declared.

4. Who, next to Korah named, his ruin shared,

5. Seditious boaster, whom Gamaliel mentions.

6. Here, blindness foiled Elisha's foes' intentions.

HOW ABOUT THAT!

"Within the covers of the Bible are all the answers for all the problems men face. The Bible can touch hearts, order minds and refresh souls."

—PRESIDENT RONALD REAGAN

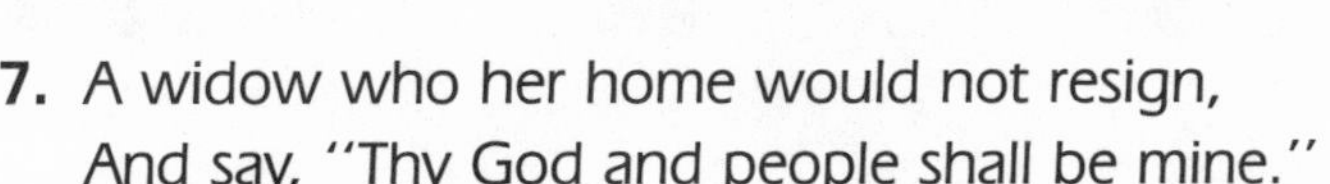

7. A widow who her home would not resign,
   And say, "Thy God and people shall be mine."

8. The priest, before whom first our Lord they took.

9. Loving this present world, who Paul forsook?

10. A word; but disentangle first the rest,
    And memory, then, this last link will suggest.

Of 1, 2, 6, 7, 8, initials two combine,
With three of 4 and 5, and one of 3 and 9.
Gracious appeal! Your highest weal at stake.
So think you well what answer you will make.

QUOTEFALL

Solve the puzzle by moving the letters to form words. The letters can only be moved to another place in the same column. Black boxes indicate the spaces between words. Each word begins in the left side of the box.

O					G	L			I		D		
A	S	U		S	L	D		E	N		T		
Y	O	B	W	I	E	E	V	I	T	N	D	O	Y
L	U	K	E	A	N	I	K	F	A	N	W	I	L
			■				■			■			
	■			■						■			■
			■					■				■	
		■					■					■	■

BIBLE CHARACTER QUIZ

Bible Character 1

I was a mother whose eagerness to secure a blessing for my son brought sorrow instead of joy! The first letter of each of the proper names described below will give you my name.

1. Whose rejection of faithful counselors led to a national rebellion?

2. To whom was the charge of the tabernacle committed during the wilderness journey?

3. The ambitious prophet who perished among the enemies of the Lord.

4. The prophet who was a witness for God before multitudes, yet fled for his life at the threat of a woman.

5. What city did David deliver from the Philistines, but its inhabitants would not protect David from the anger of Saul?

6. At what place was Israel's army first defeated after entering Canaan?

7. Whose navy was celebrated in old times, and brought great riches to Jerusalem?

ANSWERS p. 84

Bible Character 2

I am a king who set aside God's laws, and established laws of my own, to gain the affections of my people.

The first letter of each of proper names described below will give you my name:

1. The father of a king beloved of God.

2. One of the river boundaries of the Promised Land.

3. The dwelling-place of one who served God, and judged Israel all his life.

4. A deliverer and judge of Israel's people.

5. The mother of Israel's mightiest monarch.

6. The king of one of the nations destroyed by God's command when Israel entered Canaan.

7. One who took a principal part in bringing the ark of God out of the Philistine's land.

8. A Jew who rose to great honors in a foreign court.

Bible Character 3

I am a flourishing church of Asia Minor. The first letter of each of the proper names described below will give you my name.

1. A Christian householder.
2. A kinsman of St. Paul.
3. One of the divisions of the Holy Land mentioned in the New Testament.
4. A place where St. Paul was in peril from his own countrymen.
5. An eloquent man, and one mighty in the Scriptures.
6. A city from which St. Paul narrowly escaped with his life.
7. The first fruits of Achaia.
8. One of the apostles.
9. A comforter and helper of St. Paul.
10. A political sect among the Jews.
11. A division of the Roman army.
12. A New Testament prophet.

Bible Character 4

I am a man who left his native city when famine arose. The first letter of each of the proper names described on the next page will give you my name.

1. One of the brothers of the king of Israel, famous for his commanding stature.

2. The original name of the city of Dan.

3. The district in Palestine likened to an ass bowing down between two burdens.

4. The burial-place of a patriarchal family.

5. An Ethiopian who delivered a prophet from danger.

6. The mountain that the Hebrew lawgiver prayed to see.

7. The seaport where a royal fleet was wrecked.

8. A king prophesied of by name.

9. The rebuilder of Jericho.

SAYINGS ABOUT LOVE

Each of the following citations about love was written by one of the following authors: Peter, Paul, James, the author of Hebrews, or John. Can you assign the correct author to each of these quotations?

1. "But also for this very reason, giving all diligence, add to your faith virtue, to virtue knowledge, to knowledge self-control, to self-control perseverance, to perseverance godliness, to godliness brotherly kindness, and to brotherly kindness love."

2. "As many as I love, I rebuke and chasten. Therefore be zealous and repent."

3. "Let brotherly love continue. Do not forget to entertain strangers, for by so doing some have unwittingly entertained angels."

4. "And we know that all things work together for good to those who love God, to those who are the called according to His purpose."

5. "Beloved, let us love one another, for love is of God; and everyone who loves is born of God and knows God. He who does not love does not know God, for God is love. In this the love of God was manifested toward us, that God has sent His only begotten Son into the world, that we might live through Him. This is love, not that we loved God, but that He loved us and sent His Son to be the propitiation for our sins. Beloved, if God so loved us, we also ought to love one another."

HOW ABOUT THAT!

The Gutenberg Bible, 1452, was the first book printed in movable type. Fifty-six copies are known—13 in this country. Charles Scribner's Sons of New York own a fine copy that is valued at over $200,000.

6. "Since you have purified your souls in obeying the truth through the Spirit in sincere love of the brethren, love one another fervently with a pure heart, having been born again, not of corruptible seed but incorruptible, through the word of God which lives and abides forever."

7. "Nevertheless I have this against you, that you have left your first love."

8. "Blessed is the man who endures temptation; for when he has been approved, he will receive the crown of life which the Lord has promised to those who love Him."

9. "Listen, my beloved brethren: Has God not chosen the poor of this world to be rich in faith and heirs of the kingdom which He promised to those who love Him?"

10. "Greet one another with a kiss of love. Peace to you all who in Christ Jesus. Amen."

TRUE OR FALSE?

1. The word "messiah" means "anointed."

2. When Jesus met with his disciples after his resurrection, they shared a meal of lamb and bitter herbs.

3. Jesus took none of the disciples with him when he went to the Garden of Gethsemane to pray.

Q. Who introduced salted meat to the Navy?

A. Noah. He took Ham on the ark.

4. After Andrew found Jesus, he searched for his brother, Peter.

5. When Jesus said, "of such is the kingdom of God," he was referring to his apostles.

6. Peter did not want Jesus to wash his feet.

7. Jesus taught, "Do not worry about the past."

8. The Gospels of Mark and John do not record the birth of Jesus.

9. In the Gospels, Jesus is often referred to as the "Son of David."

10. Jesus spoke of separating the sheep from the wolves.

ANSWERS TO: WHO?

MULTIPLE CHOICE

#	ANSWER	REFERENCE
1.	b.	John 2:1–11
2.	d.	Matthew 8:14–17; Mark 1:29–34; Luke 4:38–41
3.	b.	Matthew 8:23–27; Mark 4:35–41; Luke 8:22–25
4.	a.	Mark 5:21–43; Luke 8:40–56
5.	d.	Matthew 14:13–21; Mark 6:30–44; Luke 9:10–17; John 6:1–14
6.	c.	Matthew 14:22–33
7.	b.	Matthew 17:1–13; Mark 9:2–13; Luke 9:28–36
8.	e.	John 9:1–41
9.	b.	John 11:1–44
10.	e.	Mark 10:46–52

FILL IN THE BLANKS

#	ANSWER	REFERENCE
1.	Joseph of Arimathea	Mark 15:42–46; Luke 23:50–53; John 19:38–42
2.	Jewish law	Luke 23:56; John 19:42
3.	Roman soldiers	Matthew 27:62–66
4.	Spices	Mark 16:1; Luke 24:1
5.	Mary Magdalene	Mark 16:9; John 20:13–18
6.	Risen	Matthew 28:6; Mark 16:6; Luke 24:6
7.	Peter, John	John 20:1–10
8.	Feel the nail prints with his own hands	John 20:25
9.	Make disciples	Matthew 28:19
10.	"with you always, even unto the end of the age"	Matthew 28:20

BIBLE
MATH

ANSWER

1. Seals in Revelation + 1 = 8 = H

   New Testament books – 6 = 21 = U

   Tribes of Israel + 1 = 13 = M

   Snakes in Eden × 2 = 2 = B

   Peter's denials × 4 = 12 = L

   Commandments ÷ 2 = 5 = E

   Years in wilderness – 21 = 19 = S

2. Number of Gospels + 1 = 5 = E

   Apostles × 2 = 24 = X

   Jesus' days in the tomb – 2 = 1 = A

   The commandments + 2 = 12 = L

   Noah's days of rain ÷ 2 = 20 = T

   Days of creation – 2 = 5 = E

   Trinity + 1 = 4 = D

He who H U M B L E S himself will be

E X A L T E D !

TRUE OR FALSE

#	ANSWER	REFERENCE
1.	False; Peter and Andrew	Matthew 4:18–19
2.	True	Matthew 6:38
3.	True	Matthew 6:9–13
4.	False; Parables	
5.	True	
6.	False; The Prodigal Son and the Wise and Foolish Virgins	Matthew 25:1–13; Luke 15:11–32
7.	False; A religious sect that criticized Jesus. Jesus considered many of them to be hypocrites	
8.	True	Matthew 14:25; Mark 6:48; John 6:19
9.	False; "Jesus wept"	John 11:35
10.	True	John 11:35

Q. Who holds the high jump record in the Bible?

A. Jesus, when he cleared the temple!

CROSSWORD PUZZLE

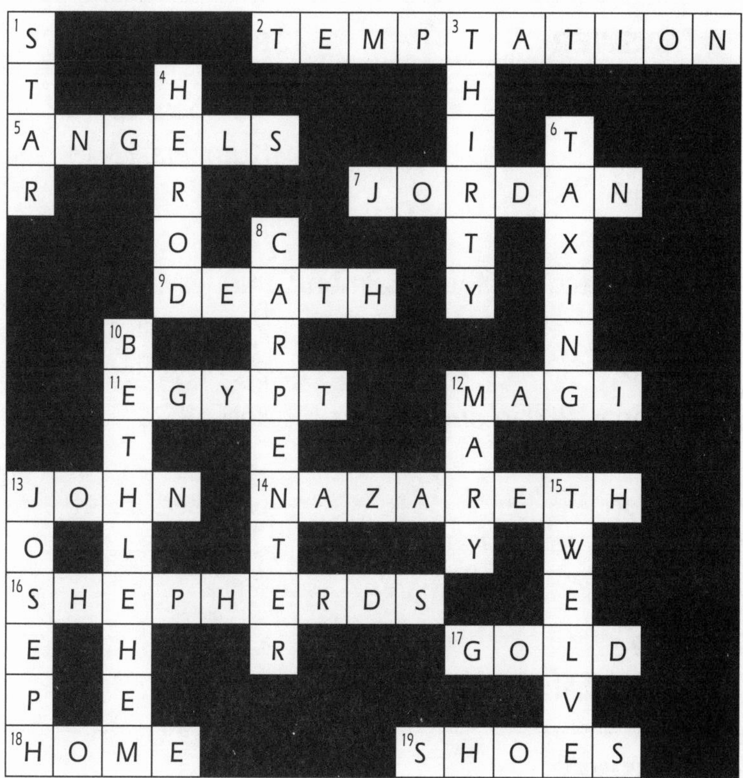

SHORT ANSWER

# ANSWER	REFERENCE
1. Men of Shechem	Judges 9:24
2. Abimelech	Judges 9:53
3. Hezekiah	2 Kings 20:6

SHORT ANSWER—cont'd

#	ANSWER	REFERENCE
4.	Balaam	Numbers 23:10
5.	Vopshi Vashni Vashti	Numbers 13:14
6.	Abimelech at Mount Zalmon	Judges 9:48
7.	Joash	2 Chronicles 23:11
8.	Ahaz	2 Chronicles 28:24
9.	Zophar, Bildad and Eliphaz by Job	Job 13:26
10.	Aaron	Numbers 16:48

WORD SCRAMBLE

#	ANSWER
1.	Isaac
2.	Sarah
3.	Moses
4.	Jacob
5.	Noah
6.	Adam
7.	Joseph
8.	Rachel

#	ANSWER
9.	Abraham
10.	Abel
11.	Miriam

BIBLE JEOPARDY

#	ANSWER
1.	What is "forsook him"?
2.	Who is Pilate?
3.	What is "crucify him"?
4.	What is Good Friday?
5.	What is Calvary?
6.	What is three hours?
7.	Who are his mother and Mary Magdalene?
8.	Who is John?
9.	What is three P.M.?
10.	What is thirty-three years old?

MATCHING

#	ANSWER	REFERENCE
1.	c.	Joshua 9:27
2.	b.	Exodus 17:8, 13
3.	g.	1 Kings 18:4

MATCHING—cont'd

#	ANSWER	REFERENCE
4.	h.	Genesis 1:9
5.	e.	Jeremiah 19:9
6.	h.	Jeremiah 20:4
7.	e.	Jeremiah 20:4
8.	f.	2 Chronicles 24:4, 11
9.	i.	Genesis 27:46
10.	a.	Joshua 7:21

WORD FIND

After finding the Matriarchs' names in the puzzle, the letters left over spell the puzzle's answer.

M	O	Ⓔ	T	Ⓗ	Ⓐ	Ⓔ	Ⓛ	Ⓑ
H	Ⓥ	Ⓘ	Ⓜ	Ⓞ	Ⓐ	Ⓝ	E	Ⓐ
Ⓔ	R	Ⓖ	Ⓞ	Ⓜ	Ⓔ	Ⓡ	S	Ⓣ
A	Ⓩ	Ⓘ	Ⓟ	Ⓟ	Ⓞ	Ⓡ	Ⓐ	Ⓗ
Ⓗ	R	Ⓨ	E	A	Ⓔ	Ⓐ	Ⓑ	Ⓢ
Ⓐ	Ⓐ	B	Ⓡ	Ⓑ	L	Ⓒ	Ⓘ	Ⓗ
Ⓝ	E	Ⓖ	Ⓔ	Ⓐ	S	Ⓗ	Ⓖ	Ⓔ
Ⓝ	S	Ⓚ	Ⓐ	I	Ⓜ	Ⓔ	Ⓐ	Ⓑ
Ⓐ	Ⓐ	N	G	Ⓡ	❤	Ⓛ	Ⓘ	Ⓐ
Ⓗ	Ⓣ	Ⓔ	Ⓑ	Ⓐ	Ⓩ	Ⓘ	Ⓛ	Ⓔ

Abigail	Rachel
Bathsheba	Hannah
Rebekah	Eve
Elizabeth	Leah
Zipporah	Naomi
Gomer	Hagar
Mary	

M O T H E R S   A R E   A

B L E S S I N G ❤

ENIGMA NO. 1

#	ANSWER	REFERENCE

"MY PEACE I GIVE UNTO YOU." John 14:27.

1.	**M**-icah	Micah 5:2
2.	**Y**-ea	2 Corinthians 1:20
3.	**P**-aul	1 Corinthians 9:1
4.	**E**-mmaus	Luke 24:13 31
5.	**A**-saph	2 Chronicles 29:30
6.	**C**-ornelius	Acts 10
7.	**E**-agle	Deuteronomy 32:11, 12
8.	**I**-ttai	2 Samuel 15:19–22
9.	**G**-alilee	Isaiah 9:1, 2; Matthew 4:12–16
10.	**I**-saiah	Isaiah 6:6–8
11.	**V**-ine	John 15:5
12.	**E**-benezer	1 Samuel 7:12
13.	**T**-erah	Genesis 11:27
14.	**O**-ded	2 Chronicles 28:9–15
15.	**Y**-ear of jubilee	Leviticus 25:8–17; Isaiah 61:1, 2
16.	**O**-badiah	2 Chronicles 17:7–9
17.	**U**-pharsin	Daniel 5:5, 25–28

ENIGMA NO. 2

#	ANSWER	REFERENCE

Revelation 3:20

"Behold, I STAND AT THE DOOR AND KNOCK. If anyone hears My voice and opens the door, I will come in to him and dine with him, and he with Me."

#	ANSWER	REFERENCE
1.	**IS**-sachar	Genesis 30:17, 18
2.	**TA**-rshish	Jonah 1:3, 4
3.	**N**-athaniel	John 1:47
4.	**DAT**-han	Numbers 16:1, 31–33
5.	**THE**-udas	Acts 5:34, 36
6.	**DO**-than	2 Kings 6:18
7.	**OR**-pah	Ruth 1:8, 14–16
8.	**AN**-nas	John 18:13
9.	**D**-emas	2 Timothy 4:10
10.	**KNOCK**	

Q. Who was the first space traveler?

A. Elijah: He went up in a fiery chariot.

QUOTEFALL

~~O~~					~~G~~	~~L~~			~~I~~		~~D~~		
~~A~~	~~S~~	~~U~~		~~S~~	~~L~~	~~D~~		~~E~~	~~N~~		~~T~~		
~~Y~~	~~O~~	~~B~~	~~W~~	~~I~~	~~E~~	~~E~~	~~V~~	~~I~~	~~T~~	~~N~~	~~D~~	~~O~~	~~Y~~
~~L~~	~~U~~	~~K~~	~~E~~	~~A~~	~~N~~	~~I~~	~~K~~	~~F~~	~~A~~	~~N~~	~~W~~	~~I~~	~~L~~
A	S	K	■	A	N	D	■	I	T	■	W	I	L
L	■	B	E	■	G	I	V	E	N	■	T	O	■
Y	O	U	■	S	E	E	K	■	A	N	D	■	Y
O	U	■	W	I	L	L	■	F	I	N	D	■	■

BIBLE CHARACTER QUIZ

Bible Character 1—REBEKAH

# ANSWER	REFERENCE
Genesis 27:6–46.	
1. **R**-ehoboam	1 Kings 12:13, 19
2. **E**-leazar	Numbers 4:16
3. **B**-alaam	Numbers 21:8
4. **E**-lijah	1 Kings 18:22; 19:2, 3
5. **K**-eilab	1 Samuel 23:12
6. **A**-i	Joshua 7:5
7. **H**-iram	1 Kings 9:27, 28

Bible Character 2—JEROBOAM

# ANSWER	REFERENCE
1 Kings 12:26–33	
1. **J**-esse	1 Samuel 17:58
2. **E**-uphrates	Joshua 1:4
3. **R**-amah	1 Samuel 7:15–17
4. **O**-thniel	Judges 3:9, 10
5. **B**-athsheba	1 Kings 2:13
6. **O**-g	Numbers 21:33–35
7. **A**-hio	2 Samuel 6:3
8. **M**-ordecai	Esther 9:4

Bible Character 3—PHILADELPHIA

# ANSWER	REFERENCE
Revelation 1:11	
1. **P**-hilemon	Philemon 1:2
2. **H**-erodion	Romans 16:11
3. **I**-turaea	Luke 3:1
4. **L**-ystra	Acts 14:19
5. **A**-pollos	Acts 18:24
6. **D**-amascus	2 Corinthians 11:32, 33
7. **E**-penetus	Romans 16:5
8. **L**-ebbaeus	Matthew 10:3
9. **P**-hebe	Romans 16:1. 2
10. **H**-erodians	Matthew 22:16

#	ANSWER	REFERENCE
11.	**I**-talian Band	Acts 10:1
12.	**A**-gabus	Acts 21:10

Bible Character 4—ELIMELECH

#	ANSWER	REFERENCE
Ruth 1:2		
1.	**E**-liab	1 Samuel 16:6, 7
2.	**L**-aish	Judges 18:29
3.	**I**-ssachar	Genesis 49:14
4.	**M**-achpelah	Genesis 23:17
5.	**E**-bed-melech	Jeremiah 38:7–13
6.	**L**-ebanon	Deuteronomy 3:25
7.	**E**-zion-geber	1 Kings 22:48
8.	**C**-yrus	Isaiah 44:28
9.	**H**-iel	1 Kings 16:34

SAYINGS ABOUT LOVE

#	ANSWER	REFERENCE
1.	Peter	2 Peter 1:5–7
2.	John	Revelation 3:19

SAYINGS ABOUT LOVE—cont'd

#	ANSWER	REFERENCE
3.	The unnamed author of Hebrews	Hebrews 13:1–2
4.	Paul	Romans 8:28
5.	John	1 John 4:7–11
6.	Peter	1 Peter 1:22–23
7.	John	Revelation 2:4
8.	James	James 1:12
9.	James	James 2:5
10.	Peter	1 Peter 5:14

TRUE OR FALSE

#	ANSWER	REFERENCE
1.	True	
2.	False; Fish and bread	John 21:9
3.	False; Peter, James, and John	Mark 14:32
4.	True	John 1:40–42
5.	False; He was referring to "little children"	Matthew 19:14

#	ANSWER	REFERENCE
6.	True	John 13:8
7.	False; He taught, "Do not worry about tomorrow."	Matthew 6:34
8.	True	
9.	True	
10.	False; From the goats	Matthew 25:32–33

What?

MULTIPLE CHOICE

1. **What miracle led to the dispersion of humankind over the entire world?**
   A. The confusion of tongues
   B. The flood
   C. The destruction of Jerusalem
   D. The plague after the time of David's census

2. **What men refused to give bread to fainting soldiers?**
   A. The Egyptians to Moses and the children of Israel
   B. Men of Succoth to Gideon's army
   C. The Men in Black
   D. People of Jerusalem to the Babylonian army

3. **What army fled in confusion when none pursued?**
   A. The Egyptian army
   B. The Salvation army
   C. The Assyrian army
   D. The Babylonian army

ANSWERS p. 117

4. **What is Isaiah's list of a woman's wardrobe?**
   A. Jingling anklets, scarves, crescents; pendants, bracelets, and veils; headdresses, leg ornaments, and headbands; perfume boxes, charms, and rings; nose jewels, festal apparel, and mantles; as well as outer garments, purses, and mirrors; and fine linen, turbans, and robes
   B. Too long to be written in one book

C. Two turbans, golden sandals, a silken robe, and earrings
D. Virtue and faithfulness

5. **What article of clothing was the token of a father's partiality?**
A. A headdress given by Isaac to Jacob
B. A coat or tunic of many colors given to Joseph by Jacob
C. Three hundred-year-old underwear given by Methuselah to his grandson
D. A fine robe given by David to Absalom

6. **What garment was hidden in a rock on the bank of the river Euphrates?**
   A. A coat of many colors
   B. A turban
   C. A sash
   D. A camel hair cloak

7. **What departing nation borrowed garments from their enemies?**
   A. The Assyrians from the Israelites
   B. The Aborigenes from the Australians
   C. The Hebrews from the Amorites
   D. The Hebrews from the Egyptians

ANSWERS
p. 117

8. **What kind of trees were the Israelites forbidden to cut down for use in a siege. Why?**
   A. Trees that produce edible fruit; they are man's life
   B. Oak trees; they are needed for firewood
   C. Cypress trees; they are needed for the construction of ships
   D. Evergreen trees; they are used on holy days

9. **What was the last of the ten plagues of Egypt?**
   A. Locusts
   B. Death of the first born
   C. Darkness
   D. Excessive dandruff

10. **In what book are there warnings against bad company?**

A. Proverbs
B. Psalms
C. Ecclesiastes
D. Isaiah

FILL IN THE BLANKS

In John's first letter and in the Letter to the Hebrews we have additional statements of who Jesus is. Can you fill in the blanks?

1. "Whoever believes that Jesus is ________________ is born of God, and everyone who loves Him who begot also loves Him who is begotten of Him."

2. "For in that He Himself has suffered, being tempted, He is ________________ those who are tempted."

3. "Therefore He is also ________________ to the uttermost those who come to God through Him, since He always lives to make intercession for them."

Q. What is the major difference between Jesus and Jonah?

A. Jesus had dinner with a sinner, and the fish had a sinner for dinner.

4. "But now He has obtained a more excellent ministry, inasmuch as He is also ________________, which was established on better promises."

5. "And for this reason He is the ________________, by means of death, for the redemption of the transgressions under the first covenant, that those who are called may receive the promise of the eternal inheritance."

The Death and Resurrection of Jesus Christ, Christian Corner Bible Quiz, by Guy de Blank, adapted by LDS.

WORD BANK

Mediator of the new covenant

able to save   able to aid

the Christ   Mediator of a better covenant

BIBLE MATH

Meeting Jesus changed people's lives! Find out how this New Testament author met Jesus by solving the puzzle the next page. Each answer is a number that matches a letter of the alphabet (A=1, B=2, C=3 . . .). Put that letter in the blank next to the number and then in the quote at the bottom to find the missing words. The first one is done for you.

ANSWERS p. 118

1st Word

Apostles + 4	=	16	=	P
Days the sun stood still	=	___	=	___
New Testament Books – 6	=	___	=	___
Bowls in Revelation + 5	=	___	=	___

2nd Word

Verses in Jude – 3	=	___	=	___
Abraham's angelic visitors × 3	=	___	=	___
Noah's days of rain – 21	=	___	=	___
Days of Unleavened Bread + 2	=	___	=	___
Spies sent into Canaan + 3	=	___	=	___
Rebekah's sons × 7	=	___	=	___

3rd Word

Steps of Solomon's throne × 3	=	___	=	___
Gold Dishes in Ezra 1 ÷ 2	=	___	=	___
Lazarus' sisters – 1	=	___	=	___
Chariots in Zechariah 6	=	___	=	___

4th Word

Jesse's sons ÷ 2 = ___ = ___

Days Paul was blind – 2 = ___ = ___

Springs at Elim + 1 = ___ = ___

Lot's daughters – 1 = ___ = ___

Chapters in Micah + 12 = ___ = ___

Jesus' days in the tomb = ___ = ___

Men cast into fiery furnace × 7 = ___ = ___

Horns of the Beast + 9 = ___ = ___

P ___ ___ ___ met Jesus in a

___ ___ ___ ___ ___ ___ on the ___ ___ ___ ___ to

___ ___ ___ ___ ___ ___ ___ ___ ___.

TRUE OR FALSE?

1. The word "Ichabod" refers to an illness mentioned in Exodus and was applied to leprosy by Moses.

2. The name of God does not appear in two books of the Bible.

3. God always uses men or weather as instruments of His anger.

4. King Solomon paid 150 shekels for a horse from Egypt.

5. Elijah's dying gift to Elisha was his mantle.

6. God manifested His presence at the dedication of the temple through an earthquake and thunder.

7. The Bible mentions only one occasion in which rain was sent in answer to prayer.

8. Once rain was prevented from falling through the prayer of Elijah.

9. God used visions sent to Moses to guide the children of Israel during their forty years' wanderings in the wilderness.

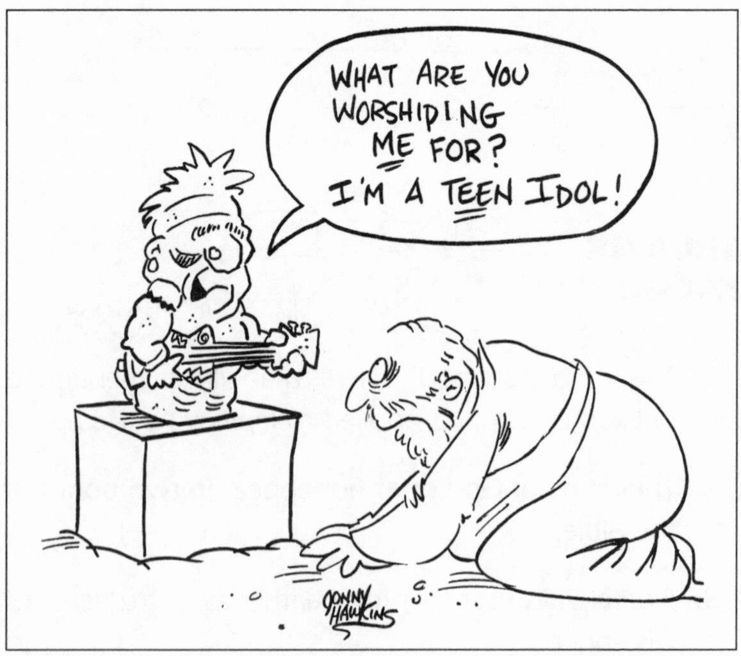

10. The first wedding present mentioned in the Bible consisted of food and cooking utensils.

CROSSWORD PUZZLE

■	■	1	2		3	4	5		6	7	■	■
■	8			■	9			■	10		11	■
12				13	■		■	14				15
	■	■	■		■		■		■	■	■	
16	17	18	■		■	■	■		■	19	20	
21			■	22					■	23		
24			■		■	■	■		■	25		
	■	■	■		■	26	■		■	■	■	
27	28	29	30		■		■	31	32	33	34	
■	35			■	36		37	■	38			■
■	■	39									■	■

Across

1. Book of ceremonial law
8. The second son of Aram and a grandson of Shem (Genesis 10:23)
9. Something dipped in liquid
10. Steal
12. River in Mesopotamia

ANSWERS p. 121

14. Joash was murdered here
16. City of Jesus' youth (abbrev.)
19. Derisive exclamation
21. A son of Benjamin; also called Ahiram (Genesis 46:21; Numbers 26:38)
22. Land of Hebrew captivity
23. A son of Zophah and a descendant of Asher (1 Chronicles 7:37)
24. Name of a family of temple servants (Nehemiah 7:47)
25. A son of Bela (1 Chronicles 7:7)
27. A son of Abraham and Keturah; Abraham's concubine (1 Chronicles 1:32)
31. Wife of Abraham
35. Last book of the New Testament (abbrev.)
36. The fifth son of Gad and leader of the Erites (Genesis 46:16; Numbers 26:16)
38. First three letters of day of rest
39. Resident of ancient city of Phrygia (central Asia Minor)

Down

1. Ancient Bethel
2. The valley where David killed Goliath
3. First two letters of name of major prophet
4. Sepulcher
5. Initial point; innings pitched; intermediate pressure
6. A temple gatekeeper who, at Ezra's urging, divorced the wife whom he had married during the Captivity (Ezra 10:24)

7. Israel's wise king (abbrev.)
8. First word of Isaiah 55
11. Barrel (abbrev.)
12. First book
13. City to which Jonah was sent
14. Belonging to the sister of Mary and Lazarus
15. Fourth minor prophet
17. A son of Abdiel, of the tribe of Gad (1 Chronicles 5:15)
18. A Gadite who lived in Bashan (1 Chronicles 5:13)
19. A son of Shemer, of the tribe of Asher (1 Chronicles 7:34)
20. Aaron died here
26. First four letters of the medical treatment of old age
28. 60 minutes (abbrev.)
29. A son of Bani who married a Gentile wife and then divorced her after the Captivity (Ezra 10:34)
30. Sargon II, king of Assyria, brought settlers from this city to colonize Samaria after the nation of Israel fell to his forces (2 Kings 17:24)
32. He led many religious reforms, "banished the perverted person from the land," and tore down pagan images and idols (1 Kings 15:12)
33. Went faster than a run
34. Jewish month
36. An altar built by the Reubenites, Gadites, and the half-tribe of Manasseh who settled east of the Jordan River (Joshua 22:34)
37. Suffix meaning "pertaining to"

SHORT ANSWER

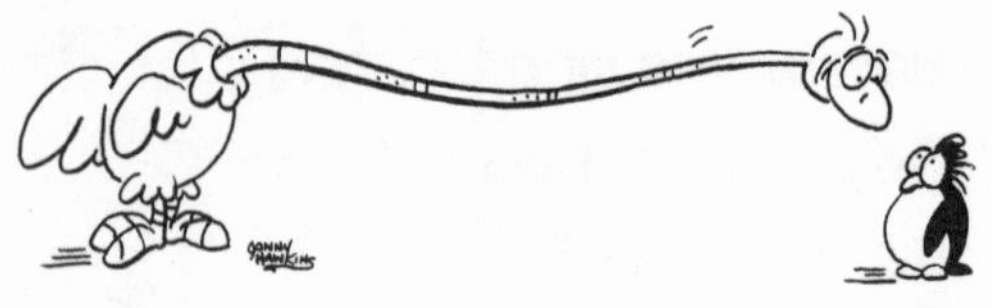

1. What early Christian church set the brightest example of liberality? ____________

2. What was the text of our Savior's first sermon?

____

3. What does the Bible tell us to contend earnestly for? ____________

4. What are we told in the Scriptures to covet?

____

5. In what way does Christ say we may know the truth of his doctrine? ____________

6. What is the unpardonable sin? ____________

7. In what place were the early disciples of Christ first called Christians? ____________

8. For what were the Bereans commended? ____________

____

9. What three New Testament instances do we have of miraculous light? ____________

10. What are three Old Testament examples of God causing people to sleep? ______________________

11. What Scripture text states that the earth is God's footstool? ______________________

12. What miracles performed by Jesus were miracles of creation? ______________________

13. What passage in the New Testament states that "every kind of beast and serpent is capable of being tamed"? ______________________

14. What is the Bible inventory of the Christian's treasure? ______________________

15. Curiosity of the eye, through the mercy of God, led to the belief of the heart when what man climbed what object? ______________________

____

WORD SCRAMBLE

What are the gifts of the Holy Spirit? Unscramble each of the words below to name them

1. SMOWID _ _ _ _ _ _
2. EWLEKONDG _ _ _ _ _ _ _ _ _
3. ITAFH _ _ _ _ _
4. ILANEHG _ _ _ _ _ _ _
5. ERACIMLS _ _ _ _ _ _ _ _
6. CHROPPEY _ _ _ _ _ _ _ _ _
7. ENGUTOS _ _ _ _ _ _ _
8. NISRENIDCG _ _ _ _ _ _ _ _ _ _

ANSWERS p. 123

BIBLE JEOPARDY

$100	$200	$300	$400	DAILY DOUBLE	$500	$600	$700	$800	$900

Here are the answers. Do you know the questions?

1. This was the sign of God's covenant with Noah.
2. This was the age of Sarah when she died.
3. This is the first commandment with a promise.
4. This is the first book of the Bible named for a woman.
5. This is the first tree definitely named in the Bible.
6. This church, named in Revelation, had left its first love.
7. This was the first of the plagues that God visited upon Egypt.
8. This prompted Christ to say, "If any man desires to be first, the same shall be last of all, and servant of all."

Q. During what season did Eve eat the forbidden fruit?

A. Early in the fall.

MATCHING

Each of these questions is followed by an answer but most of the answers are to the wrong questions. Can you straighten them out?

1. What does the Bible declare to be the whole duty of man?	a. "You shall love your neighbor as yourself."
2. What in the Bible is called the "royal law"?	b. Ruling one's spirit.
3. In what time period did God send rain as a sign of his displeasure against Israel?	c. In the days of the prophet Samuel.
4. What does the Bible say is better than precious ointment?	d. The tablets of stone.
5. What is it that makes its possessor truly rich?	e. Death.
6. What is a greater conquest than the taking of a city?	f. The blessing of the Lord.
7. What was found in the Ark of the Covenant when it was first brought into the temple?	g. A good name.
8. What was the divinely appointed punishment for blasphemy?	h. Fear God and keep his commandants.

ANSWERS p. 124

9. What is the number of witnesses required among the Jews to establish a charge?

i. Seven.

10. What number of Sabbaths is mentioned in the Bible?

j. Two or three.

WORD FIND

Find the books of the Bible in the puzzle. Some are in a straight line up and down, some left to right, on an angle (and backwards, of course). Circle each letter of each word. The letters remaining spell out the secret puzzle message.

H	A	I	D	A	B	O	J	O	H	N
A	A	G	O	L	U	K	E	D	S	O
I	M	N	H	E	B	R	E	W	S	M
M	W	O	O	O	O	A	R	D	G	E
E	I	S	S	J	A	M	E	S	E	L
R	E	V	E	L	A	T	I	O	N	I
E	Z	R	A	R	E	H	T	S	E	H
J	T	C	R	E	X	O	D	U	S	P
U	T	I	T	U	S	H	A	C	I	M
S	N	A	I	S	E	H	P	E	S	E

Acts
Amos
Esther
Ezra
Exodus
Ephesians
Genesis
Hebrews
Hosea
James
Jeremiah
Job
Joel
John
Jonah
Luke
Mark
Micah
Obadiah
Philemon
Revelation
Titus

___'_ ______ __ ____.

ENIGMA NO. 1

1. Word that God alone can claim.
2. A slave who won a dearer name.
3. A holy woman raised to life.
4. A man who took a gleaner wife.
5. A feast of triumph after pain.
6. The robe that martyr myriads gain.
7. The name that "laughter" does express.
8. A bishop charged to faithfulness.
9. A counselor and faithful friend.
10. A thing once yours, forever gone.
11. A name of Christ that means "the end"
12. The light from Aaron's breastplate thrown.

Q. What was one of the first example of math in the Bible?

A. God told Adam to go forth and multiply.

In these initials does there lie,
The full form of the word "good-bye."

ENIGMA NO. 2

1. What office did our Lord fulfill in offering Himself as a sacrifice for sin?

2. What expression is used concerning Christ, as of the house of David?

3. In what term does St. Paul, in his epistle to the Corinthians, speak of the relation of Christ to the Father?

4. What title of Christ, though given to him in contempt by his enemies, was the fulfillment of a prophecy?

5. A name of our Savior that indicates his wisdom?

6. In what prophetic language is the essential attribute of God ascribed to Christ?

7. A title by which our Lord's human descent is described.

8. Under what designation does prophecy indicate Christ as "cleansing from all iniquity"?

9. Name the grand office of Christ as our Divine Teacher.

10. What prophetic title of our Savior shows Him to be both God and Man?

11. One of our Savior's names taken from the Greek alphabet.

12. How does our Lord show Himself to be the support of that temple built up of his elect?

HOW ABOUT THAT!

The Song of Solomon is the one book of the Bible dedicated solely to romantic love. Isn't it ironic that its initials are SOS?

—Paul McGinty

13. What is it that Christ's people find in Him?

From these initials you will find
The love of God to humankind.
He sent his Son from heaven on high,
For us to suffer, bleed, and die.
Oh, happy time, when He shall come
To bring us to our heavenly home.
The war, and strife, and sin shall cease,
And Jesus come to reign in peace.

QUOTEFALL

Solve the puzzle by moving the letters to form words. The letters can only be moved to another place in the same column. Black boxes indicate the spaces between words. Each word begins in the left side of the box.

	L			T		E			L		D				O			T	V					
A	L			F		H	E		T		E		I	S	C	R		A	M	E	D			W
N	N	O	I	E		W	I	L	L	A	R	A	S	I	E	M	I	I	A	I	T	H		E
N	D	D	R	S	A	W	E	L	R	H	Y	E	C	O	M	F	G	F	N	E	U	T	S	A
I	S	L	H	D	H	V	I	P	H	A	B	E	R	F	O	K	H	I	T	D	N	P	H	I
			■				■							■			■						■	
			■					■				■					■				■			
■					■					■						■				■			■	
		■			■			■				■										■		
		■			■					■			■									■	■	■

CRAZY QUOTATIONS

ANSWERS p. 127

Not everything is as it appears. And not everything that is said is clearly understood. One sage advises: "Never trust a thing that you see and only half of what you hear." Can you decode these two confused quotes and tell what the Bible really says? [Hing: It helps if you read them aloud.]

1. "But as it is written:
   'Rye is not beans, nor steer herd,
   Nor have entered into the hearth of Van
   The sandwich Cod has preplanned for toads with relish.'"

2. "And He said to me, 'My grave is forbidden for you, for My strength is maids' perfect impassive.' Therefore most gladly I will rather boat my infirmaries, that the powder of grist may roast up on my knee."

3. "Though I speak with the mugs of ten, but Havelock Ellis, I have become pounding grass or a changing limbo. And though I have the gift of Pro Football, and underplan tall miseries and tall college, and though I have tall feet, so that I could retail Fun Trains, but have hot rugs, I am mutton."

4. "I have been beautified to a crisp; it is no longer Iowa, but crisp leaves Indy. . . ."

5. "And He Himself gave some to be epistles, some profits, some old tennis guides, and some bleaters and beaters, for the blue striping of the ants for the world of mimicry, for the head-defying of the bottle too crisp."

6. "Bear on your brother durbans, and so fill full the jaw of mice."

7. "Do not be believed, Don is not knocked; for what sweater Emil shows, that he with salsa heaps."

8. "Sit on the role rumor of Todd that you weigh stables to sand against the walls of the double. For tea settle against food and blips, but against Prince, Pal E, against Fido, against the dog food of the barking of the pups, against empirical boasts of hiddeness in the leisurely paces."

9. "Fortunately, to live is crime, and to dye again."

10. "Re-juice in the orange always. Again I will say, re-juice!"

11. "I can do almost through grips that strengthens me."

HOW ABOUT THAT!

The Hebrew language of the Old Testament contained no vowels, only consonants, in every word.

MULTIPLE CHOICE

1. **What was manna?**
   - A. An Israelite from the tribe of Mann
   - B. A Hebrew nickname for one's grandmother
   - C. Unleavened bread used in the feast of Passover
   - D. Bread from heaven

2. **What did manna taste like?**
   - A. Chicken
   - B. Modern day pizza

ANSWERS
p. 130

C. Wafers of honey
D. A cross between mayonnaise and bananas

3. **What substitute was given to Abraham for the sacrifice of Isaac?**
   A. A ram caught in a thicket
   B. Mrs. Sawyer, third grade
   C. Thirty pieces of silver
   D. His brother, Esau

4. **Where in the Bible is the reference to "the rose of Sharon, and the lily of the valleys"?**
   A. Nowhere. It is the name of a nineteenth century novel.
   B. Song of Solomon 2:1
   C. Psalm 24:3
   D. 1 Thessalonians 4:1–2

5. **What was remarkable about Balaam's donkey?**
   A. Its dancing
   B. Its appetite
   C. It could interpret dreams and warned Pharaoh of a coming famine
   D. It saw the angel of the Lord opposing her master's way, and spoke to the prophet

Q. What did Noah say as he was loading the Ark?

A. "Now I herd everything."

6. **What lesson did Christ draw from the sparrows?**
   - **A.** That flying is better than walking
   - **B.** Man can live on worms alone
   - **C.** Look before you leap
   - **D.** That God cares for each of us

7. **In connection with what event is a broom (or juniper) tree mentioned?**
   - **A.** Sweeping the floor before the arrival of a guest
   - **B.** Absalom getting caught by his hair
   - **C.** Noah's ark was constructed from its wood
   - **D.** Elijah's despondency in the wilderness, during his flight from Jezebel

8. **What animal tempted Eve?**
   A. A box turtle
   B. A fox
   C. A serpent
   D. A spider

9. **What bird did Jesus say could not fall to the ground without God's knowledge?**
   A. Dove
   B. Sparrows
   C. Eagle
   D. Big Bird

10. **What animals did Pharaoh tell Joseph he had dreamed about?**
    A. Camels
    B. Donkeys
    C. Birds of the air
    D. Cows

ANSWERS TO: WHAT?

MULTIPLE CHOICE

#	ANSWER	REFERENCE
1.	a.	Genesis 11:6, 9
2.	b.	Judges 8:4, 6
3.	c.	2 Kings 7:39
4.	a.	Isaiah 3:18, 23
5.	b.	Genesis 37:3
6.	c.	Jeremiah 13:4
7.	d.	Exodus 12:35
8.	a.	Deuteronomy 20:19, 20
9.	b.	Exodus 11:5.10
10.	a.	Proverbs 1:10; 1:15; 4:14–15

FILL IN THE BLANKS

#	ANSWER	REFERENCE
1.	the Christ	1 John 5:1
2.	able to aid	Hebrews 2:18
3.	able to save	Hebrews 7:25
4.	Mediator of a better covenant	Hebrews 8:6
5.	the Mediator of the new covenant	Hebrews 9:15

BIBLE MATH

#	ANSWER				
1.	Apostles + 4	=	16	=	P
	Days the sun stood still	=	1	=	A
	New Testament Books – 6	=	21	=	U
	Bowls in Revelation + 5	=	12	=	L
2.	Verses in Jude – 3	=	22	=	V
	Abraham's angelic visitors × 3	=	9	=	I
	Noah's days of rain – 21	=	19	=	S
	Days of Unleavened Bread + 2	=	9	=	I
	Spies sent into Canaan + 3	=	15	=	O
	Rebekah's sons × 7	=	14	=	N
3.	Steps of Solomon's throne × 3	=	18	=	R
	Gold Dishes in Ezra 1 ÷ 2	=	15	=	O
	Lazarus' sisters – 1	=	1	=	A
	Chariots in Zechariah 6	=	4	=	D
4.	Jesse's sons ÷ 2	=	4	=	D
	Days Paul was blind – 2	=	1	=	A
	Springs at Elim + 1	=	13	=	M
	Lot's daughters – 1	=	1	=	A
	Chapters in Micah + 12	=	19	=	S

# ANSWER				
Jesus' days in the tomb	=	3	=	C
Men cast into fiery furnace × 7	=	21	=	U
Horns of the Beast + 9	=	19	=	S

P A U L met Jesus in a

V I S I O N on the R O A D to

D A M A S C U S .

TRUE OR FALSE

#	ANSWER	REFERENCE
1.	False; "The glory is departed." Phinehas' wife named her son Ichabod to mark several tragedies that had overcome her family and nation Israel.	1 Samuel 4:21
2.	True	Esther and Song of Solomon
3.	False; On four occasions he used wild animals:	
	a. A lion killed the disobedient prophet	1 Kings 13:24

TRUE OR FALSE—cont'd

#	ANSWER	REFERENCE
	b. A lion killed the man that disobeyed the prophet	1 King 20:35, 36
	c. Lions killed Daniel's enemies	Daniel 6:24
	d. Bears killed Elisha's mockers	2 King 2:24
4.	True	2 Chronicles 1:17
5.	True	2 Kings 2:13
6.	False; Fire came from heaven and consumed the sacrifice; the glory of the LORD filled the house	1 Kings 8:11; 2 Chronicles 7:1
7.	False; Two: Elijah and Samuel	1 Kings 18:42–45 1 Samuel 12:16, 18
8.	True	1 Kings 17:1
9.	False; By a pillar of cloud by day, a pillar of fire by night	Exodus 13:21
10.	False; Jewels of gold and silver and expensive clothing presented to Rebekah	Genesis 24:53

Q. What was the name of Isaiah's horse?

A. It must have been "Isme." After all he did say, "Whoa, Isme!"

CROSSWORD PUZZLE

■	■	1 L	2 E	V	3 I	4 T	5 I	C	6 U	7 S	■	■
■	8 H	U	L	■	9 S	O	P	■	10 R	O	11 B	■
12 G	O	Z	A	13 N	■	M	■	14 M	I	L	L	15 O
E	■	■	■	I	■	B	■	A	■	■	■	B
16 N	17 A	18 Z	■	N	■	■	■	R	■	19 A	20 H	A
21 E	H	I	■	22 E	G	Y	P	T	■	23 H	O	D
24 S	I	A	■	V	■	■	■	H	■	25 I	R	I
I	■	■	■	E	■	26 G	■	A	■	■	■	A
27 S	28 H	29 U	30 A	H	■	E	■	31 S	32 A	33 R	34 A	H
■	35 R	E	V	■	36 E	R	37 I	■	38 S	A	B	■
■	■	39 L	A	O	D	I	C	E	A	N	■	■

SHORT ANSWER

# ANSWER	REFERENCE
1. Macedonia	2 Corinthians 8:1, 5; Phil 4:15–18
2. Repent	Matthew 4:17
3. The faith of the saints	Jude 3
4. The best gifts	1 Corinthians 12:31

SHORT ANSWER—cont'd

#	ANSWER	REFERENCE
5.	"If anyone wants to do His will"	John 7:17
6.	To blaspheme against the Holy Spirit, e.g. by attributing the works of God to the devil.	Matthew 7:31
7.	At Antioch	Acts 11:26
8.	Searching the Scriptures	Acts 17:11
9.	Three instances:	
	a. The angel announcing the birth of Christ	Luke 2:9
	b. Paul's conversion	Acts 9:3
	c. Peter's deliverance from prison	Acts 12:7
10.	Three examples:	
	a. Adam	Genesis 2:21
	b. Abraham	Genesis 15:12
	c. Saul and his army	1 Samuel 26:12
11.	Matthew 5:35	
12.	Miracles of creation:	
	a. The turning water into wine	John 2:7, 10
	b. The feeding of the multitudes on two occasions.	Matthew 14:15, 21; 15:34–38

#	ANSWER	REFERENCE
13.	James 3:7	
14.	All things	1 Corinthians 3:21–23
15.	Zacchaeus; A tree	Luke 19:2

WORD SCRAMBLE

#	ANSWER
1.	Wisdom
2.	Knowledge
3.	Faith
4.	Healing
5.	Miracles
6.	Prophecy
7.	Tongues
8.	Discerning

BIBLE JEOPARDY

#	ANSWER	REFERENCE
1.	What is the rainbow?	Genesis 8:11–13
2.	What is 127 years old?	Genesis 23:1
3.	What is the fifth commandment?	Exodus 20:12

BIBLE JEOPARDY—cont'd

#	ANSWER	REFERENCE
4.	What is the book of Ruth?	
5.	What is the fig tree?	Genesis 2:17; 3:7
6.	What is Ephesus?	Revelation 2:4
7.	What is the river turning to blood?	Exodus 7:14–24
8.	What is the disciples disputing?	Mark 9:33–35

MATCHING

#	ANSWER	REFERENCE
1.	h.	Ecclesiastes 12:13
2.	a.	James 2:8, Leviticus 19:18
3.	c.	1 Samuel 12:18
4.	g.	Ecclesiastes 17:15
5.	f.	Proverbs 10:22
6.	b.	Proverbs 16:32
7.	d.	2 Chronicles 5:10
8.	e.	Leviticus 24:16
9.	j.	Deuteronomy 19:15
10.	i.	Hebrews 4:9; Psalm 95:11

WORD FIND

After finding the books of the Bible in the puzzle, the letters left over spell the puzzle's answer.

Ⓗ Ⓐ Ⓘ Ⓓ Ⓐ Ⓑ Ⓞ Ⓙ Ⓞ Ⓗ Ⓝ
Ⓐ Ⓐ G O Ⓛ Ⓤ Ⓚ Ⓔ D S Ⓞ
Ⓘ Ⓜ Ⓝ Ⓗ Ⓔ Ⓑ Ⓡ Ⓔ Ⓦ Ⓢ Ⓜ
Ⓜ W Ⓞ Ⓞ Ⓞ O Ⓐ R D Ⓖ Ⓔ
Ⓔ I S Ⓢ Ⓙ Ⓐ Ⓜ Ⓔ Ⓢ Ⓔ Ⓛ
Ⓡ Ⓔ Ⓥ Ⓔ Ⓛ Ⓐ Ⓣ Ⓘ Ⓞ Ⓝ Ⓘ
Ⓔ Ⓩ Ⓡ Ⓐ Ⓡ Ⓔ Ⓗ Ⓣ Ⓢ Ⓔ Ⓗ
Ⓙ T Ⓒ R Ⓔ Ⓧ Ⓞ Ⓓ Ⓤ Ⓢ Ⓟ
U Ⓣ Ⓘ Ⓣ Ⓤ Ⓢ Ⓗ Ⓐ Ⓒ Ⓘ Ⓜ
Ⓢ Ⓝ Ⓐ Ⓘ Ⓢ Ⓔ Ⓗ Ⓟ Ⓔ Ⓢ E

Acts	Job
Amos	Joel
Esther	John
Ezra	Jonah
Exodus	Luke
Ephesians	Mark
Genesis	Micah
Hebrews	Obadiah
Hosea	Philemon
James	Revelation
Jeremiah	Titus

G O D ' S W O R D I S T R U E.

ENIGMA NO. 1

# ANSWER	REFERENCE
"GOD BE WITH YOU."	
1. **G**-ood	Matthew 19:16, 17
2. **O**-nesimus	Philippians 1:16
3. **D**-orcas	Acts 9:36–41
4. **B**-oaz	Ruth 4:13
5. **E**-aster	1 Corinthians 5:7, 8
6. **W**-hite	Revelation 7:13, 14

ENIGMA NO. 1—cont'd

#	ANSWER	REFERENCE
7.	**I**-saac	Genesis 21:4, 6
8.	**T**-imothy	2 Timothy 1
9.	**H**-ushai	2 Samuel 17:5–14
10.	**Y**-esterday	Psalm 90:4
11.	**O**-mega	Revelation 22:13
12.	**U**-rim	Exodus 28:30

ENIGMA NO. 2

#	ANSWER	REFERENCE
	"PRINCE OF PEACE." Isaiah 9:6.	
1.	**P**-riest	Hebrews 5:6
2.	**R**-oot	Revelation 5:5
3.	**I**-mage of God	2 Corinthians 4:4
4.	**N**-azarene	Matthew 2:23
5.	**C**-ounsellor	Isaiah 9:6
6.	**E**-verlasting Father	Isaiah 9:6
7.	**O**-ffspring of David	Revelation 17:16
8.	**F**-ountain	Zech. 13:1
9.	**P**-rophet	Deuteronomy 18:18
10.	**E**-mmanuel	Matthew 1:23

# ANSWER	REFERENCE
11. **A**-lpha	Revelation 1:8
12. **C**-hief Corner Stone	1 Peter 2:6
13. **E**-ternal Life	1 John 5:20

QUOTEFALL

	L			T		E			L		D				O			T	V					
A	L			F		H	E		T		E		I	S	C	R		A	M	E	D			W
N	N	O	I	E		W	I	L	L	A	R	A	S	I	E	M	I	I	A	I	T	H		E
N	D	D	R	S	A	W	E	L	R	H	Y	E	C	O	M	F	G	F	N	E	U	T	S	A
I	S	L	H	D	H	V	I	P	H	A	B	E	R	F	O	K	H	I	T	D	N	P	H	I
A	N	D	■	T	H	E	■	P	R	A	Y	E	R	■	O	F	■	F	A	I	T	H	■	W
I	L	L	■	S	A	V	E	■	T	H	E	■	S	I	C	K	■	A	N	D	■	T	H	E
■	L	O	R	D	■	W	I	L	L	■	R	A	I	S	E	■	H	I	M	■	U	P	■	A
N	D	■	I	F	■	H	E	■	H	A	S	■	C	O	M	M	I	T	T	E	D	■	S	I
N	S	■	H	E	■	W	I	L	L	■	B	E	■	F	O	R	G	I	V	E	N	■	■	■

CRAZY QUOTATIONS

# ANSWER	REFERENCE
1. "But as it is written: 'Eye has not seen, nor ear heard, Nor have entered into the heart of man the things which God has prepared for those who love Him.'"	1 Corinthians 2:9

CRAZY QUOTATIONS—cont'd

# ANSWER	REFERENCE
2. "And He said to me, 'My grace is sufficient for you, for My strength is made perfect in weakness.' Therefore most gladly I will rather boast in my infirmities, that the power of Christ may rest upon me."	2 Corinthians 12:9
3. "Though I speak with the tongues of men and of angels, but have not love, I have become sounding brass or a clanging cymbal. And though I have the gift of prophecy, and understand all mysteries and all knowledge, and though I have all faith, so that I could remove mountains, but have not love, I am nothing."	1 Corinthians 13:1–2
4. "I have been crucified with Christ; it is no longer I who live, but Christ lives in me;	Galatians 2:20

#	ANSWER	REFERENCE
	and the life which I now live in the flesh I live by faith in the Son of God, who loved me and gave Himself for me."	Galatians 2:20
5.	"And He Himself gave some to be apostles, some prophets, some evangelists, and some pastors and teachers, for the equipping of the saints for the work of ministry, for the edifying of the body of Christ."	Ephesians 4:11,12
6.	"Bear one another's burdens, and so fulfill the law of Christ."	Galatians 6:2
7.	"Do not be deceived, God is not mocked; for whatever a man sows, that he will also reap."	Galatians 6:7
8.	"Put on the whole armor of God that you may be able to stand against the wiles of the devil. For we do not wrestle against flesh and	Ephesians 6:11–12

CRAZY QUOTATIONS—cont'd

#	ANSWER	REFERENCE
	blood, but against principalities, against powers, against the rulers of the darkness of this age, against spiritual hosts of wickedness in the heavenly places."	Ephesians 6:11–12
9.	"For to me, to live is Christ, and to die is gain."	Philippians 1:21
10.	"Rejoice in the Lord always. Again I will say, rejoice!	Philippians 4:4–7
11.	"I can do all things through Christ who strengthens me."	Philippians 4:13

MULTIPLE CHOICE

#	ANSWER	REFERENCE
1.	d.	Exodus 16:1–15
2.	c.	Exodus 16:31
3.	a.	Genesis 22:13
4.	b.	Song of Solomon 2:1
5.	d.	Numbers 22:22–31

#	ANSWER	REFERENCE
6.	d.	Matthew 11:29
7.	d.	1 Kings 19:4
8.	c.	Genesis 3:1–2
9.	c.	Matthew 10:29–31
10.	d.	Genesis 41:14–24

When?

MULTIPLE CHOICE

1. When was consuming fire quenched in answer to prayer?

A. When Moses interceded with the LORD.
B. When Mount Sinai erupted.
C. When Joshua asked the LORD for a sign.
D. When Elijah called down fire from heaven.

ANSWERS p. 163

2. When did an apostle exhort two women to agree?

A. When Peter settled an argument between Mary and Martha.
B. When Paul was attempting to make peace among the Philippians.
C. When John urged Mary, the mother of the Lord, and Mary Magdalene not to argue over the body of Jesus.
D. When James ordered Eunice and Lois to come to terms.

3. When was an invading army first blinded, and then fed?

A. When Joab's army attempted to arrest David.
B. When they came to capture Elisha.
C. When Abner's army attempted to kill Joab.
D. When the Babylonians invaded Jerusalem.

4. When was water mistaken for blood just before a battle?

A. When the Syrians saw the sea at sunset.

B. When the Egyptians thought the Nile had turned to blood.

C. When the Assyrian thought he had a glass of water.

D. When the Moabites saw the morning sun reflected on the water.

5. **When did a foreign commander shout in Hebrew to Jews on the wall of Jerusalem?**
   A. Five years ago.
   B. When the Moabites attacked the city.
   C. When the Rabshakeh, Assyrian military officials, spoke.
   D. When the Arabian raiders attacked the city.

6. **When was a sound in the treetops a battle signal to a king?**
   A. In the movie, *Willow.*
   B. When Samson attacked the Philistines.
   C. When the LORD told David when to attack.
   D. When Saul attacked the Moabites.

7. **When did one prophet smite another prophet on the cheek?**
   A. When Zedekiah struck Micaiah and accused him of being a liar.
   B. When Elijah and Elisha argued.
   C. When Samuel corrected Eli.
   D. When Jeremiah prophesies about Baruch's mother.

8. **When were twenty-four young men slain in combat just before a battle?**
   A. When a tournament of champions was held before the battle between the forces of Ishbosheth and the forces of David.
   B. When David and his brothers killed Goliath and his men.

C. When Goliath killed the champions of Israel.
D. When Samson smote the Philistines.

9. **When did one man's avarice bring about the defeat of an army?**
   A. When Joab demanded a reward of David.
   B. When David taxed his people.
   C. When Solomon demanded tribute of the Syrians.
   D. When Achan took booty contrary to the commandment of God.

10. **When were mirrors turned to use for the worship of God?**
    A. When they were used to reflect the sunrise after the last day of Passover.
    B. When Moses used them to signal the time to cross the Red Sea.
    C. When the priests used them to make sure that their vestments were spotless.
    D. When Bezalel made the laver of bronze and its base of bronze from the bronze mirrors of the serving women who assembled at the door of the tabernacle of meeting.

FILL IN THE BLANKS

1. Jesus taught that Christians should wash their faces before ____________.

2. Women helped to rebuild the walls of __________.

3. David killed ______________________ when he wanted to marry Bathsheba.

4. The prophet __________ was commanded to shave his head and beard.

5. __________ advised a man's five daughters to all marry their cousins, and so inherit their father's land.

6. The prophet __________ purchased a field while he was shut up in prison.

7. Hannah, a devout woman, was mistaken for a drunkard when she was __________.

8. __________ was the first convert from Europe.

9. __________, the priest, wept while he was praying.

10. __________ told the shepherds to howl and cry and wallow in ashes when it was their turn to be slaughtered or dispersed.

Q. When did Moses sleep with five people at once? **A. When he slept with his fore fathers**	

WORD BANK

Lydia	Jeremiah	Moses
fasting	Ezra	praying
Uriah the Hittite		Jerusalem
Ezekiel	Jeremiah	

BIBLE MATH

When we put our trust in God He can do amazing things through us! Find out what happened to a small shepherd boy who trusted God by solving the puzzle below. Each answer is a number that matches a letter of the alphabet (A=1, B=2, C=3 . . .). Put that letter in the blank next to the number and then in the quote at the bottom to find the missing words. The first one is done for you.

1st Word

People in Eden × 2	= 4	= D
Gospels – 3	= ___	= ___
Silver pieces paid to Judas – 8	= ___	= ___
Sons of Noah × 3	= ___	= ___
Heads of the Beast	= ___	= ___

2nd Word

Plagues on Egypt + 1	= ___ = ___
Letters to Timothy + 7	= ___ = ___
Jesus' age when he taught at Temple	= ___ = ___
Elders in Revelation ÷ 2	= ___ = ___
Chapters in Micah – 2	= ___ = ___
Tribes of Israel ÷ 3	= ___ = ___

3rd Word

Wings of a "Living Creature" + 1	= ___ = ___
Plagues in Revelation + 8	= ___ = ___
Jairus's daughters age	= ___ = ___
Jesse's sons + 1	= ___ = ___
Men crucified with Jesus – 1	= ___ = ___
Old Testament books – 10	= ___ = ___
Josiah's age when crowned king	= ___ = ___

4th Word

Silver paid for Joseph – 1	= ___ = ___
Lazarus' sisters X 6	= ___ = ___
Lepers who didn't thank Jesus	= ___ = ___
Chapters in Judges – 7	= ___ = ___
Sons of Heman ÷ 2	= ___ = ___
Beatitudes + 9	= ___ = ___

Days before a boy is circumcised = ___ = ___

Days Joshua circled Jericho + 8 = ___ = ___

Spies hidden by Rahab × 10 = ___ = ___

D___ ___ ___ ___ ___ ___ ___ ___ ___ ___ ___

___ ___ ___ ___ ___ ___ ___ ___ with only a

___ ___ ___ ___ ___ ___ ___ ___ ___ ___.

TRUE OR FALSE?

1. Ezekiel wore a yoke upon his neck to symbolize the conquests of Nebuchadnezzar, the king of Babylon.
2. Elisha healed a spring of polluted water by throwing salt in it.
3. When the descendants of Joseph were attacking Bethel, a man saved his life by betraying his city.
4. When Elijah was demonstrating God's promise, fire destroyed silver and gold.
5. When Pharaoh disregarded Moses' plea and locusts invaded Egypt, the country was delivered by a west wind.
6. When a funeral was interrupted by armed raiders, a dead man thrown into Elisha's grave came to life.
7. A miracle of loaves and fishes performed by Elisha enabled a widow to pay her debts.

8. As Elisha was dying, King Joash wept over him.

9. Four hundred single men found wives at a dance.

10. When the LORD caused the Aramean army to hear a sound like that of chariots, they regained their courage and fought bravely.

CROSSWORD PUZZLE

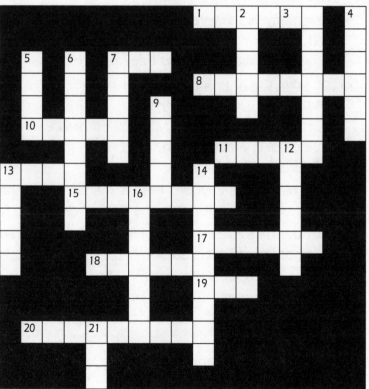

ANSWERS p. 167

Across

1. For 450 years the land of Israel was governed by whom? (Acts 13:20)
7. The longest drought recorded in the Bible was three years and __________ months. (Luke 4:25)
8. How many years did it take Solomon to build his house? (1 Kings 7:1)
10. For how many days did the children of Israel journey in the wilderness before they found water? (Exodus 15:22)
11. In __________-two days the walls of Jerusalem were rebuilt. (Neh. 6:15)
13. How many years were required to elapse, according to the law of Moses, before the Israelites might gather the fruit of a young tree? (Lev. 19:25)
15. For how many years was Israel oppressed by the Ammonites? (Judges 10:8)
17. For how many years had Moses lived before he demanded of Pharaoh that the children of Israel should go? (Exodus 7:7)
18. What place where Moses lived is mentioned in the New Testament, but not in the Old? (Acts 7:30)
19. For how many years did Paul live in his own hired house at Rome? (Acts 28:30)
20. One of the reasons the children of Israel wandered in the wilderness. (Numbers 14:33)

Down

2. For seven years and six months, __________ reigned over Judah alone in Hebron. (2 Samuel 2:11)

3. For____________ years, the children of Israel were in exile in the lands of Babylon. (Jeremiah 25:11)
4. For a hundred and ____________ years, God gave warning to the people of the old world before sending the flood. (Genesis 6:3)
5. When Eli was 98, he fell from his ____________ and died. (1 Samuel 4:15)
6. On what day of the first month of the year was the Passover lamb or goat appointed to be slain? (Exodus 12:6)
7. For how many days did the first plague sent by God upon the Egyptians last? (Exodus 7:25)
9. In what land did the children of Israel live before the Exodus?
12. The children of Israel sojourned in Egypt for four hundred and ____________ years. (Exodus 12:40)
13. After his great troubles, Job lived for a hundred and ____________ years. (Job 42:16)
14. How old was Joseph when his brothers sold him into slavery? (Genesis 37:2)
16. The flood at the time of Noah covered the earth for one-____________ and fifty days. (Genesis 7:24)
21. Where did Noah stay for 150 days? (Genesis 7:24)

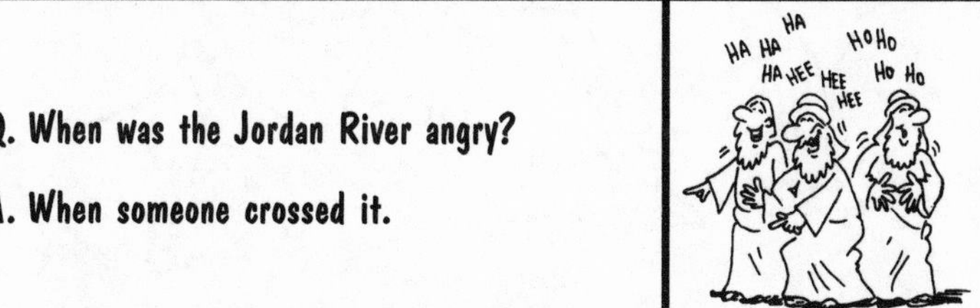

Q. When was the Jordan River angry?

A. When someone crossed it.

SHORT ANSWER

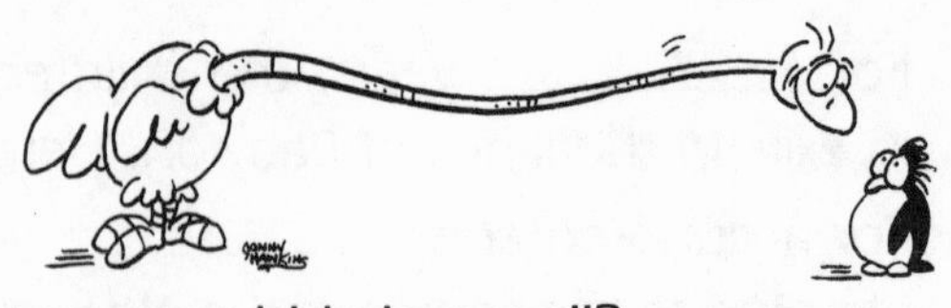

1. When did two men hide in a well? ____________

____

2. When did more than forty men take an oath to go on a hunger-strike until they had committed a murder? ____________________________

3. When did a servant gain freedom, according to Old Testament laws on personal injuries? ____________

____

4. When did a Hebrew captain receive an omen of victory through an enemy's dream? ______________

____

HOW ABOUT THAT!

The Bible is not only the best selling book of all time, it is also the best selling book EVERY year!

5. When was a mother paid for nursing her own baby?

____

6. When did an earthquake open the doors of a prison? ______________________________

7. When were ten people killed by a tornado while they feasted together? ______________________________

8. When did thunder win a battle for a discouraged army? ______________________________

9. When did 185,000 soldiers die in a single night?

____

10. When did postmen ride in on riding on royal horses bred from swift steeds? ___________________

WORD GAME

As Christians, we recognize that the Lord is King of this earth and all its creatures. In the puzzle below, make the Lord the King in just six simple steps. On each line change only one letter to form a different, actual word. To help, the letter that changes has been marked with a star.

Ex.: C A N
C A T
C O T
H O T

L O R D

_ _ _ _ (*4th letter)

_ _ _ _ (*3rd letter)

_ _ _ _ (*4th letter)

_ _ _ _ (*1st letter)

_ _ _ _ (*2nd letter)

K I N G

ANSWERS p. 169

BIBLE JEOPARDY

$100	$200	$300	$400	DAILY DOUBLE	$500	$600	$700	$800	$900

Here are the answers. Do you know the questions?

1. God commanded Ezekiel to tell one (Ezekiel 17:1–2).
2. Zedekiah did so to predict the destruction of the Syrians (1 Kings 22:11).
3. When King Asa dismantled Ramah. (1 Kings 15:17, 21, 22).
4. To pay the king's tax (Nehemiah 5:3).
5. When they were conveying the Ark of the Covenant (1 Chronicles 13:7–9).
6. When Jonathan promised to protect David (1 Samuel 23:16–18).
7. Hananiah the prophet after being cursed by Jeremiah (Jeremiah 28:15–17).
8. When the angel appeared to Manoah (Judges 13:18).
9. When her son Micah stole her money (Judges 17:2).
10. When Elisha guided the king's hands (2 Kings 13:15–17).
11. When Paul led them through the ritual of purification (Acts 21:23–27).

12. By Jesus to the Apostles, as they shared a meat "after his resurrection and just previous to his ascension (Mark 16:14–15).

13. Paul and his companions before the shipwreck (Acts 27:37).

MATCHING

1. When was a king cured of disease by means of a poultice of figs?

2. When did a priest ask for a writing-table?

3. When was poisoned stew made wholesome by adding meal?

4. When was a king discovered asleep with his spear stuck in the ground?

5. When did a victorious captain accept from his soldiers a trophy consisting of golden earrings?

6. When did envoys disguise themselves by wearing old clothes?

a. When Elisha was entertaining a group of prophets

b. When the body was placed in the tomb of Elisha

c. When Gideon saved the Israelites from the Midianites

d. When Israel tried to find favor with Joseph

e. When Paul was arrested

f. When Isaiah treated King Hezekiah

7. When was a corpse revived by contact with a prophet's bones?

8. When did a present consist of honey, spices and myrrh, pistachio nuts and almonds?

9. When was a sermon preached on a staircase?

10. When was a prisoner guarded by 470 soldiers?

g. When a speechless Zacharias insisted that this son be named John

h. When David came upon Saul

i. When the inhabitants of Gibeon heard how Joshua had dealt with Jericho and Ai.

j. When Paul preached while he was held captive in Jerusalem

WORD FIND

Find each of the words mentioned in Genesis in the puzzle below. Some are in a straight line up and down, some left to right, some on an angle (and backwards, of course). Circle each letter of each word.

M	E	G	S	I	H	A	K	E	B	E	R
G	A	V	P	E	L	E	A	R	S	I	A
E	R	D	E	H	T	O	F	I	V	R	U
N	B	S	A	N	A	H	G	X	K	A	A
E	Y	E	J	B	E	E	U	J	S	B	A
S	W	R	O	C	E	D	L	E	E	B	L
I	O	P	S	C	L	N	E	L	R	A	E
S	B	E	E	Z	E	S	J	A	C	E	H
Q	N	N	P	L	H	N	H	A	K	W	C
H	I	T	H	A	I	A	Z	I	M	K	A
U	A	Q	O	A	M	Q	F	S	M	I	R
J	R	N	C	F	A	M	I	N	E	Q	N

Abel	Cain	Genesis	Rachel
Abraham	Eden	Israel	Rainbow
Adam	Esau	Joseph	Rebekah
Ark	Eve	Leah	Serpent
Benjamin	Famine	Noah	Seth

ENIGMA NO. 1

ANSWERS
p. 172

Combine the initials of these royal names;

> They give a text which man's poor splendor shames.
> In summer glory God the earth arrays,
> And crowns with beauty the succeeding days.
> Go, walk the fields and breathe the fragrant air
> And mark the perfect wisdom everywhere
> What palace is there like the vaulted sky?

1. The king whom Abram slew to save Lot's life.
2. The king whose son took Jezebel to wife.
3. The king whose pride by God was brought down low.
4. The king who, fearful, to a witch did go.
5. The king's son who was murdered on his bed.
6. The king who mourned in song his foe when dead.
7. The king who to Jehoiachin was kind.

Q. To what question could Eve never say yes?

A. When Adam asked if she had heard his jokes from anyone else.

8. The king who would not aged counselors mind.
9. The king whose warlike help King Ahaz prayed.
10. The king who begged that God would grant him aid.
11. The king who cruelly died by Ehud's blade.
12. The king whose mother words of wisdom taught.
13. The king's court that the gentle Esther sought.
14. The king-built city where the king was slain.
15. The king's consoler sent to ease his pain.
16. The king whose brothers twain their father slew.
17. The king who, more than any, heavenly wisdom knew.

Source: Cliff Leitch, http://www.twopaths.com.

ENIGMA NO. 2

ANSWERS p. 172

Note: Answer is a single word.

It is a word I love to hear,
Though not of English birth.
A gentle word that fitly falls,
From hapless sons of earth.
From patient souls that seek and love
The help that comes from God above.

No plainer words, no simpler words,
To baby lips belong;
For turn this way, or turn it that,
You cannot turn it wrong.
And yet the holiest lips were heard
To utter first this simple word.

Two letters make this simple word,
But oh, how much they mean.
They touch our earth, they soar to heaven,
They span the gulf between.
And when its mission here is o'er,
This word shall reach the further shore.

QUOTEFALL

ANSWERS p. 173

Solve the puzzle by moving the letters to form words. The letters can only be moved to another place in the same column. Black boxes indicate the spaces between words. Each word begins in the left side of the box.

I			D				B			N								
N	D		T	H	E		W	O	R	I	T	W	A	G	T	H	O	A
W	N	T	H	E	E	W	S	R	G	D	N	N	I	N	G	G	W	D
S	O	R	T	H	W	A	O	E	W	I	A	H	D	S	O	D	E	A
		■				■										■		
	■				■					■				■				■
				■				■					■				■	
		■				■					■				■			

MULTIPLE CHOICE

1. **Of the books of the New Testament, which was the first to be written?**
   A. Matthew
   B. Mark
   C. Luke
   D. First Thessalonians
   E. Chicken Soup for the Soul

2. **Of the four Gospels, Matthew, Mark, Luke and John, which was written first?**
   A. Matthew
   B. Mark
   C. Luke
   D. John
   E. Jeff

3. **Of the four Gospels, Matthew, Mark, Luke and John, which is the last written?**
   A. Matthew
   B. Mark
   C. Luke
   D. John
   E. Bubba

4. **Which three New Testament books are known as the "Synoptic Gospels?"**
   A. Matthew, Mark and Luke
   B. Luke, John and Acts
   C. Mark, Luke and John

D. Matthew, Luke and John
E. Acts, Romans, and Galatians

5. **The Vulgate was the standard Bible of Christianity for many centuries. In what language was it written?**
   A. Greek
   B. Latin
   C. Canadian
   D. English
   E. Partially in Hebrew; partially in Aramaic

ANSWERS
p. 173

6. **What was the name of the first Bible printed on a printing press?**
   A. King James Version
   B. Revised Standard Version
   C. The Geneva Bible
   D. The Gutenberg Bible
   E. The Beta Version

7. **In what year was this first Bible published?**
   A. 1389
   B. 1456
   C. 1477

My ten-year-old nephew Michael's version of John 3:16: "For God so loved the world that He gave His only begotten Son, that whoever believes in Him should not perish but have ever-laughing life."

D. 1501
E. 1965

8. **The first English translation of the Bible dates from:**
   A. 1115
   B. 1384
   C. 1611
   D. 1821
   E. 1950

9. **The King James Version of the Bible was published in what year?**
   A. 1384
   B. 1611
   C. 1758
   D. 1903
   E. 1580

10. **How many languages has the Bible been translated into?**
    A. Over 500
    B. Over 1000
    C. Over 1500

Q. At what time was Adam born?

A. A little before Eve.

D. Over 2000
E. about 4

Cliff Leitch (<http://www.twopaths.com/>http://twopaths.com) as adapted by LDS.

SHORT ANSWER

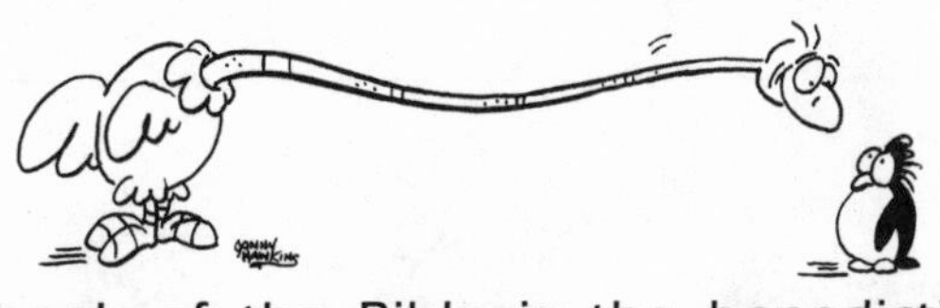

1. In what book of the Bible is the benediction beginning, "Now to Him who is able to keep you from stumbling"? ______________________

2. Repeat Christ's saying about idle words. ______________________

3. Who wrote, "The just shall live by faith," and in what book is it found? ______________________

4. What is said in Hebrews about Christ's temptations and sinlessness? ______________________

5. How did James define religion? ______________________

6. Quote exactly the angels' Christmas song at Bethlehem. ______________________

7. What is the most quoted verse in the Bible? ______________________

8. In Christ's parable, what happened to the seeds that fell on stony ground? ______________________

9. In Christ's parable, what happened to the seeds that fell on the good ground? ______________________

10. What does James call "the royal law"? __________

____

TRUE OR FALSE

1. Isaiah, the Old Testament prophet, wrote, "The just shall live by his faith." James, a New Testament writer, insisted on the same doctrine.

2. When he stilled the tempest, Christ said, "Peace, be still."

3. On the Sabbath, when He healed the man with a withered hand, Christ asked, "Is it lawful on the Sabbath days to do good, or to do evil?"

4. On the same occasion Christ said, "My Father has been working until now, and I have been working."

HOW ABOUT THAT!

The only domestic animal not mentioned in the Bible is the cat.

5. Jesus and John the Baptist said that God "dwells not in temples made with hands."

6. Christ said that healing and casting out evil spirits is "the work of God".

7. When the apostles were bringing a donkey for Jesus to ride into Jerusalem on, they said, "It is hard for you to kick against the goads".

8. Jesus warned that unclean food and drink are the kinds of things that defile a person.

9. With the words, "Tabitha, arise," Peter raised Dorcas from the dead.

10. Jesus said that his "food" was "bread and water."

ANSWERS TO: WHEN?

MULTIPLE CHOICE

# ANSWER	REFERENCE
1. a.	Numbers 11:2
2. b.	Philippians 4:2
3. b.	2 Kings 6:13–23
4. d.	2 Kings 3:21–24
5. c.	2 Kings 18:26,28
6. c.	2 Samuel 5:22–25
7. a.	1 Kings 22:24
8. a.	2 Samuel 2:12–17
9. d.	Joshua 7
10. d.	Exodus 38:8

FILL IN THE BLANKS

# ANSWER	REFERENCE
1. fasting	Matthew 6:17
2. Jerusalem	Nehemiah 3:12
3. Uriah the Hittite	2 Samuel 11:1–27
4. Ezekiel	Ezekiel 5:1
5. Moses	Numbers 36:1–12
6. Jeremiah	Jeremiah 32:6–12

FILL IN THE BLANKS—cont'd

#	ANSWER	REFERENCE
7.	praying	1 Samuel 1:12–15
8.	Lydia	Acts 16:14,15, 40
9.	Ezra	Ezra 10:1
10.	Jeremiah	Jeremiah 25:34

BIBLE MATH

#	ANSWER		
1.	People in Eden × 2	= 4	= D
	Gospels – 3	= 1	= A
	Silver pieces paid to Judas – 8	= 22	= V
	Sons of Noah × 3	= 9	= I
	Heads of the Beast	= 4	= D
2.	Plagues on Egypt + 1	= 11	= K
	Letters to Timothy + 7	= 9	= I
	Jesus' age when he taught at Temple	= 12	= L
	Elders in Revelation ÷ 2	= 12	= L
	Chapters in Micah – 2	= 5	= E
	Tribes of Israel ÷ 3	= 4	= D

#	ANSWER				
3.	Wings of a "Living Creature" + 1	=	7	=	G
	Plagues in Revelation + 8	=	15	=	O
	Jairus's daughters age	=	12	=	L
	Jesse's sons + 1	=	9	=	I
	Men crucified with Jesus – 1	=	1	=	A
	Old Testament books – 10	=	20	=	T
	Josiah's age when crowned king	=	8	=	H
4.	Silver paid for Joseph – 1	=	19	=	S
	Lazarus' sisters X 6	=	12	=	L
	Lepers who didn't thank Jesus	=	9	=	I
	Chapters in Judges – 7	=	14	=	N
	Sons of Heman ÷ 2	=	7	=	G
	Beatitudes + 9	=	19	=	S
	Days before a boy is circumcised	=	8	=	H
	Days Joshua circled Jericho + 8	=	15	=	O
	Spies hidden by Rahab X 10	=	20	=	T

D A V I D K I L L E D

G O L I A T H with only a

S L I N G S H O T.

TRUE OR FALSE?

#	ANSWER	REFERENCE
1.	False; Jeremiah	Jeremiah 27:2; 28:10
2.	True	2 Kings 2:19–22
3.	True	Judges 1:23–25
4.	False; The fire consumed wood, stones, dust, and water.	1 Kings 18:38
5.	True	Exodus 10:13–19
6.	True	2 Kings 13:20–21
7.	False; Elisha filled a widow's vessels with oil.	2 Kings 4:1–7
8.	True	2 Kings 13:14
9.	True; When the men of Benjamin sought replacements for their wives who had been killed	Judges 21:20–23
10.	False; They were put to flight.	2 Kings 7:6–7

Q. Was there any money on the ark?

A. Yes: The duck took a bill, the frog took a green back, and the skunk took a scent.

CROSSWORD PUZZLE

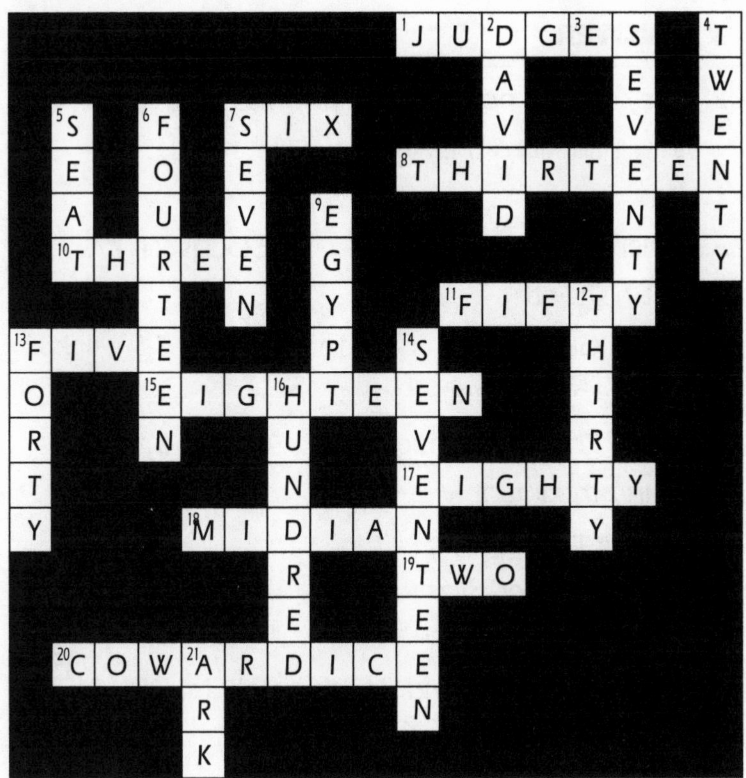

SHORT ANSWER

#	ANSWER	REFERENCE
1.	Jonathan and Ahimaaz hid in a well when avoiding capture by Absalom's men.	2 Samuel 17:18, 19

SHORT ANSWER—cont'd

#	ANSWER	REFERENCE
2.	They vowed not to eat until they had killed the Apostle Paul.	Acts 23:12–14
3.	When his master knocked out his tooth.	Exodus 21:27
4.	When Gideon was about to attack the Midianite forces.	Judges 7:9—15:31
5.	When Pharaoh's daughter found the infant Moses in the reeds along the Nile.	Exodus 2:9
6.	When Paul and Silas were imprisoned in Philippi.	Acts. 16:26
7.	When Job's sons and daughters were feasting together.	Job 1:1,18,19
8.	When the thunder frightened the Philistines as they prepared to fight the Israelites	1 Samuel 7:7–11
9.	The night before the Assyrians were ready to attack.	2 Kings 19:35
10.	When King Ahasuerus sent a message to the Jews.	Esther 8:10

WORD GAME

ANSWER

L O R D

L O R E*

L O N* E

L O N G*

S* O N G

S I* N G

K I N G

BIBLE JEOPARDY

ANSWER

1. When was a prophet commanded to put forth a riddle?
2. When did a prophet make iron horns to enforce his message?
3. When was a newly built city dismantled, and its stones and timber taken away to build two other cities?
4. When were certain Jews driven to mortgage their lands and houses to buy food?

BIBLE JEOPARDY—cont'd

#	ANSWER
5.	When did two men drive oxen pulling a new cart?
6.	When did two men make a covenant in the wilderness?
7.	When did a false prophet die a few months after a true prophet had foretold his death?
8.	When did an angel refuse to tell his name because it was secret?
9.	When did a woman utter curses because she had been robbed?
10.	When did a prophet help to shoot an arrow?
11.	When did four men shave their heads?
12.	When, where, by whom and to whom was the command given, "Go to all the world and preach the gospel"?
13.	When did two hundred and seventy-six distressed persons, before day-break, partake of a joyful meal?

MATCHING

#	ANSWER	REFERENCE
1.	f.	Isaiah 38:21–22
2.	g.	Luke 1:60–66

# ANSWER	REFERENCE
3. a.	2 Kings 4:38–41
4. h.	1 Samuel 26:11–25
5. c.	Judges 7
6. i.	Joshua 9:1–7
7. b.	2 Kings 13:20–21
8. d.	Genesis 43:11–13
9. j.	Acts 21:39–40
10. e.	Acts 23:23–24

WORD FIND

Ⓜ Ⓔ G Ⓢ I Ⓗ Ⓐ Ⓚ Ⓔ Ⓑ Ⓔ Ⓡ
Ⓖ Ⓐ Ⓥ P Ⓔ Ⓛ Ⓔ Ⓐ Ⓡ Ⓢ Ⓘ Ⓐ
Ⓔ R Ⓓ Ⓔ Ⓗ Ⓣ O F I V Ⓡ Ⓤ
Ⓝ B Ⓢ Ⓐ Ⓝ Ⓐ Ⓗ G X Ⓚ Ⓐ Ⓐ
Ⓔ Y Ⓔ Ⓙ Ⓑ Ⓔ Ⓔ U J Ⓢ Ⓑ Ⓐ
Ⓢ Ⓦ Ⓡ Ⓞ C Ⓔ Ⓓ Ⓛ Ⓔ Ⓔ Ⓑ Ⓛ
Ⓘ Ⓞ Ⓟ Ⓢ C L Ⓝ Ⓔ Ⓛ Ⓡ A Ⓔ
Ⓢ Ⓑ Ⓔ Ⓔ Z E S Ⓙ Ⓐ C E Ⓗ
Q Ⓝ Ⓝ Ⓟ L Ⓗ Ⓝ Ⓗ Ⓐ K W Ⓒ
H Ⓘ Ⓣ Ⓗ Ⓐ Ⓘ Ⓐ Z I Ⓜ K Ⓐ
U Ⓐ Q Ⓞ Ⓐ Ⓜ Q F S M Ⓘ Ⓡ
J Ⓡ Ⓝ Ⓒ Ⓕ Ⓐ Ⓜ Ⓘ Ⓝ Ⓔ Q Ⓝ

ENIGMA NO. 1

#	ANSWER	REFERENCE

"CONSIDER THE LILIES." Matthew 6:28.

#	Answer	Reference
1.	**C**-hedorlaomer	Genesis 14:17
2.	**O**-mri	1 Kings 16:28
3.	**N**-ebuchadnezzar	Daniel 4:33
4.	**S**-aul	1 Samuel 28:8
5.	**I**-shobosheth	2 Samuel 4:7
6.	**D**-avid	2 Samuel 1:17
7.	**E**-vil-merodach	Jeremiah 52:31–34
8.	**R**-enoboam	1 Kings 12:8
9.	**T**-iglath-pileser	2 Kings 16:7
10.	**H**-ezekiah	2 Kings 19:15–19
11.	**E**-glon	Judges 3:21, 25
12.	**L**-emuel	Proverbs 31:1
13.	**I**-nner court	Esther 5:1
14.	**L**-achish	2 Chronicles 11:9; 25:27
15.	**I**-saiah	2 Kings 20:5–7
16.	**E**-sarhaddon	Kings 21:37
17.	**S**-olomon	2 Chronicles 1:12

ENIGMA NO. 2

ANSWER

"ABBA." Mark 14:36; Romans 8:15; Galatians 4:6

QUOTEFALL

I			D				B			N								
N	D		T	H	E		W	O	R	I	T	W	A	G	T	H	O	A
W	N	T	H	E	E	W	S	R	G	D	N	N	I	N	G	G	W	D
S	O	R	T	H	W	A	O	E	W	I	A	H	D	S	O	D	E	A
I	N	■	T	H	E	■	B	E	G	I	N	N	I	N	G	■	W	A
S	■	T	H	E	■	W	O	R	D	■	A	N	D	■	T	H	E	■
W	O	R	D	■	W	A	S	■	W	I	T	H	■	G	O	D	■	A
N	D	■	T	H	E	■	W	O	R	D	■	W	A	S	■	G	O	D

MULTIPLE CHOICE

 # ANSWER

1. d. Though it is debatable, First Thessalonians was probably the first book to be written. It is estimated to have been written between 40–45 A.D. by Paul.
2. b. The four-source theory holds that Mark was the first gospel written. It is estimated to have been written between 60–65 A.D. based upon shorter sentence structure, fewer chapters, and quick, to-the-point written style.
3. d. John is believed to be the most recent. The argument for this is supported by the theologically advanced statements made throughout the book..

MULTIPLE CHOICE—cont'd

 # ANSWER

4. a. Matthew, Mark and Luke are known as the "Synoptic gospels." That is, literally, "seeing together," these three are similar in their writings, order of pericopes, and view of the Passion and Resurrection of Jesus..
5. b. The Vulgate was written by St. Jerome in Latin. It was considered the "vulgar" version because it was the first translation from Koine to a vernacular language.
6. d. The Gutenberg Bible was the first Bible printed on a printing press in the fifteenth century. After the technological advancements of the printing press, the gospel was more widely spread throughout the world..
7. b. 1456; This was prior to the Protestant Revolution.
8. b. 1384; John Wycliffe first translated the Bible into the English Language. Later he was burned at the stake for his commitment to Protestantism and evangelizing the gospel.
9. b. 1611: King James I first published the English version of the Bible under a Protestant reign. This version has been an authoritative work even unto today.

#	ANSWER
10.	c. Due to a commitment to spreading the good news, many missionaries and churches have aided in the process of translating the Bible into over 1500 languages. This process continues even today at different language institutes. The Bible continues to be the best selling book in the world.

SHORT ANSWER

#	ANSWER	REFERENCE
1.	Jude	Jude 24–25
2.	"But I say to you that for every idle word men may speak, they will give account of it in the day of judgment."	Matthew 12:36
3.	Paul, quoting Habakkuk 2:4.	Romans 1:17
4.	That He "was in all points tempted as we are, yet without sin."	Hebrews 4:15
5.	"Pure and undefiled religion before God the Father is this: to visit orphans and widows in	James 1:27

SHORT ANSWER—cont'd

#	ANSWER	REFERENCE
	their trouble, and to keep oneself unspotted from the world."	
6.	"Glory to God in the highest, And on earth peace, goodwill toward men!"	Luke 2:14
7.	"For God so loved the world that He gave His only begotten Son, that whoever believes in Him should not perish but have everlasting life."	John 3:16
8.	They sprang up quickly, but soon withered away.	Mark 4
9.	They yielded thirtyfold, sixtyfold, or a hundredfold.	Mark 4
10.	"You shall love your neighbor as yourself."	James 2:8

TRUE OR FALSE?

#	ANSWER	REFERENCE
1.	False; Paul	Habakkuk 2:4; Romans 1:17.
2.	True	Mark 4:39

#	ANSWER	REFERENCE
3.	True	Luke 6:6–11
4.	False; When, on the Sabbath, he healed the man at the Pool of Bethesda, and the Jews criticized him for working a cure on that day	John 5:2–17
5.	False; Stephen and Paul	Acts 7:48; 17:24
6.	False; "This is the work of God, that you believe in Him whom He sent."	John 6:29
7.	False; Saul heard these words when Christ appeared to him near Damascus.	Acts 9:5
8.	False; He said, "Not the things from without but the things from within the man."	Mark 7:15
9.	True	Acts 9:40
10.	False; He said, "My food is to do the will of him who sent me."	John 4:34

Where?

CENSUS
WHERE IS YOUR HOMELAND?
"CAN WE COUNT ON YOU?"
JONNY HAWKINS

MULTIPLE CHOICE

1. **According to the Psalms, how do mountains skip?**
   - **A.** Like goats
   - **B.** Like a sack of potatoes
   - **C.** Like rams
   - **D.** Like antelopes
   - **E.** Like children

2. **What is the name of the mountain of the Lord?**
   - **A.** Everest
   - **B.** Zion
   - **C.** Sinai
   - **D.** Hermon
   - **E.** Horeb

ANSWERS p. 208

3. **Which mountain did the ark rest on?**
   - **A.** Gerizim
   - **B.** Gilboa
   - **C.** Lebanon
   - **D.** Ararat
   - **E.** Kilamanjaro

4. **Where did Solomon build the house of the Lord?**
   - **A.** Mount Moriah
   - **B.** Mount of Olives
   - **C.** Mount Carmel
   - **D.** Mount Rushmore
   - **E.** Mount Tabor

5. **Whose army was defeated at Mount Tabor?**
   A. Sennacherib's
   B. Corilanus'
   C. Jabin's
   D. Joab's
   E. Sisera's

6. **Which of the following notable events happened at Mount Sinai?**
   A. Jesus crucified
   B. Jesus ascended
   C. Moses' first sinus attack

D. Ten commandments received
E. Joshua defeats Moab

7. **Which was the Mount of Blessing?**
   A. Gerizim
   B. Nebo
   C. Zion
   D. Olives
   E. Vernon

8. **Moses saw the Promised Land from this mountain:**
   A. Ebal
   B. Hermon
   C. Vesuvius
   D. Nebo
   E. Tabor

ANSWERS p. 208

9. **What did Joshua build on Mount Ebal?**
   A. Temple
   B. Idol
   C. Altar
   D. A Starbucks
   E. House

10. **What is an alternative name for Mount Hermon?**
    A. Zion
    B. Sirion
    C. Smyrna
    D. Sinai
    E. Larry

Source: Marc Hunter, www.biblequizzes.com.

FILL IN THE BLANKS

1. ____________ lies five miles south of Jerusalem.

2. ____________ was the first European city to hear Christian preaching.

3. The longest river in Palestine is the __________ river.

4. The Bible calls "the great river" the ____________ river.

5. The Israelites sent spies into Canaan from ________-____________.

6. After he had killed the Egyptian, Moses fled to ____________.

7. John was on the isle of ____________ when he wrote Revelation.

Q. Where is paper money mentioned in the Bible?

A. Where the dove brought a greenback to the ark.

8. Amos lived in the city of ____________, five miles south of Bethlehem.

9. Samuel's home was in ____________.

10. Jonah ran to ____________ (southern Spain) when running away from his duty, and he set sail from ____________.

WORD BANK

Tarshish	Tekoa	Jordan
Joppa	Ramah	Philippi
Bethlehem	Kadesh-barnea	
Joppa	Midian	Tekoa
Euphrates	Ramah	Patmos

BIBLE MATH

Many important Bible events took place on mountains. Fill in the puzzle to find out why this pair of mountains was important to Israel. Each answer is a number that matches a letter of the alphabet (A=1, B=2, C=3 . . .).

Put that letter in the blank next to the number and then in the quote at the bottom to find the missing words. The first one is done for you.

1st Word

Jesus' temptations + 2 = _5_ = _E_

Days Lazarus was in tomb ÷ 2 = ___ = ___

Sons of Rachel – 1 = ___ = ___

Elders in Revelation ÷ 2 = ___ = ___

2nd Word

Church letters in Revelation – 5 = ___ = ___

Lepers who didn't thank Jesus + 3 = ___ = ___

Chapters in Lamentations = ___ = ___

Horns of the Beast + 9 = ___ = ___

Verses in Philemon – 6 = ___ = ___

Commandments – 1 = ___ = ___

Ears of corn in Pharaoh's dream = ___ = ___

Jesse's sons – 1 = ___ = ___

3rd Word

Steps of Solomon's throne + 1 = ___ = ___

Psalms ÷ 30 = ___ = ___

Cities of Refuge × 3 = ___ = ___

Tribes of Israel – 3 = ___ = ___

New Testament Books – 1 = ___ = ___

Job's friends × 3 = ___ = ___

Abijah's wives – 1 = ___ = ___

4th Word

Lamech's wives + 1 = ___ = ___

Years in wilderness – 19 = ___ = ___

Years Aeneas was bedridden + 10 = ___ = ___

Silver paid for Joseph – 1 = ___ = ___

Loaves Jesus used to feed 5000 = ___ = ___

Horns of the beast + 9 = ___ = ___

Before they entered the Promised Land they had to pass between E___ ___ ___ the Mount of ___ ___ ___ ___ ___ ___ ___ ___ and ___ ___ ___ ___ ___ ___ ___ the Mount of ___ ___ ___ ___ ___ ___.

ANSWERS p. 211

TRUE OR FALSE?

1. At Jericho, the walls "came tumblin' down."
2. The final battle between good and evil will take place on Mt. Carmel.
3. The first public miracle performed by Jesus took place in Nazareth.

4. In Antioch, the disciples of Jesus were called "Christians" for the first time.

5. God frustrated the building of a temple in Babel.

HOW ABOUT THAT!

G.K. Chesterton and other literary figures were asked what book they would want to have with them if stranded on a desert island. One said without hesitation, "The complete works of Shakespeare." Another said, "The Bible." Chesterton replied, "I would choose Thomas's *Guide to Practical Ship Building.*"

6. Balaam's donky had a successful singing career throughout Samaria.

7. Joseph was sold at Mt. Moriah.

8. Edom was the land of Esau.

9. Samson "brought down the house" in Babylon.

10. Peter healed a blind man at the Beautiful Gate.

CROSSWORD PUZZLE

Across

1. Where Dorcas lived
4. On the western shore of the Sea of Galilee
8. On his way to Jerusalem, Paul met here with elders from Ephesus.
9. Divided between followers of Paul, Apollos, and Cephas

11. Where Mary and Martha lived
12. Where Paul saw his "Macedonian vision"
13. Where Christ's first miracle was performed
14. Where Peter went to live after being freed from prison
15. City from which a colt was taken
18. Seaport of Antioch
21. First European city to hear the Gospel
22. Also known as the "Mount of Olives"
23. John baptized here

Down

1. City of palm trees
2. Where John wrote Revelation
3. Its name means "Thessalonian Victory."
5. In this Syrian city, converts were urged to hold fast in their faith.
6. First of these set out from Antioch in Syria
7. Paul's home city
10. A palsied man healed by Peter
13. Barnabas' birthplace
16. Caesarea Philippi is at the foot of this mount.

Q. Where did Noah keep his bees?

A. In the Archives.

17. Country from which the Holy Family returned
19. The region we call "Asia Minor"
20. City five miles from Nazareth

SHORT ANSWER

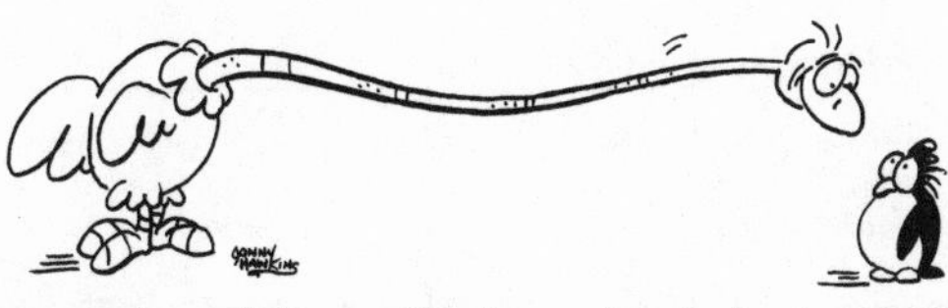

1. What is the name of the city to which Lot escaped at the destruction of Sodom? ____________________

2. Where was the voice of God first heard by human ear? ____________________

3. In what city was a forty-day fast proclaimed?
____

4. What does "a dish wiped and turned upside down" illustrate? ____________________

5. What Biblical city was known as the city of palm trees? ____________________

6. Where was Rachel buried? ____________________

7. According to prophecy, what city was destroyed and never again inhabited? ____________________

8. Where, in Scripture language, is the land of Canaan 1ocated? ____________________

9. At what seaport town was assembled the largest navy of biblical times? ____________

10. What city was saved from massacre by the strategy of its people? ____________

WORD SCRAMBLE

Where did Jesus travel during his ministry? Unscramble each of the words below to name these cities Jesus visited.

1. MAPRANCEU _ _ _ _ _ _ _ _ _
2. STADEBHIA _ _ _ _ _ _ _ _ _
3. DALGAMA _ _ _ _ _ _ _
4. TZARHANE _ _ _ _ _ _ _ _
5. HANTEBY _ _ _ _ _ _ _
6. ALERSUMJE _ _ _ _ _ _ _ _ _
7. MASUEM _ _ _ _ _ _
8. NAAC _ _ _ _
9. IZAKRON _ _ _ _ _ _ _
10. ANIN _ _ _ _
11. MLEEBTEH _ _ _ _ _ _ _ _
12. RAAGDA _ _ _ _ _ _

ANSWERS p. 213

BIBLE JEOPARDY

$100	$200	$300	$400	DAILY DOUBLE	$500	$600	$700	$800	$900

Here are the answers. Do you know the questions?

1. This is where the walls fell down.
2. A final battle occurred here, according to Revelation.
3. The first miracle of Christ happened here.
4. Disciples were first called Christians here.
5. A tower was built here, and confusion followed.
6. Paul preached here.
7. Joseph was sold here by his brothers.
8. Esau lived here.
9. Samson was carried off the city gates at this place.
10. A lame man was healed at this point by Peter.

Q. Where is medicine first mentioned in the Bible?

A. When God gave Moses two tablets.

MATCHING

1. Eden	a. Where Adam and Eve disobeyed God and were expelled
2. Mt. Ararat	b. Where Solomon built the temple
3. Haran	c. David's palace was here
4. Bashan	d. Moses died here
5. Mt. Carmel	e. The home of Laban
6. Mayberry	f. The probable other name for Mt. Hermon
7. Mt. Nebo	g. The ark landed here
8. Mt. Moriah	h. The Ten Commandments were given here
9. Mt. Sinai	i. Elijah's altars were here
10. Mt. Zion	j. Where Andy begat Opey and kept the peace with Barney

WORD FIND

Find the name of Bible places in the puzzle. Some are in a straight line up and down, some left to right, some on an angle (and backwards, of course). Circle each letter of each word. The letters left over spell out the puzzle's message.

```
G E N A A N A C
I N G M Z S I N
L O E Y O A E N
E M D N P D G E
A M O A E T O H
D A M A S C U S
L E B A B R I O
J E R I C H O G
```

Ammon	Eden
Edom	Babel
Canaan	Damascus
Egypt	Gaza
Gilead	Goshen
Jericho	Moab
Sodom	Ur

Where did Moses receive the Ten Commandments?

On Mount ___ ___ ___ ___ ___ ___.

ENIGMA NO. 1

ANSWERS p. 216

Take the initials, and, as noonday clear,
A title of the Savior will appear.

1. Whose mournful death made widows to lament?
2. What woman from her master's house was sent?
3. Who saw bright visions by a river's side?
4. What treacherous servant to his master lied?
5. What warlike prince upon a rock was slain?
6. Who sought water when God withheld the rain?

7. Who came uninjured from the lion's den?

8. Who, once near Lehi, slew a thousand men?

9. Whose prayers and tears did a kind answer gain?

10. In what famed valley was a giant slain?

11. Who, for his sin, most bitterly did weep?

12. Where did his flock the son of Amram keep?

13. Who, with a brother, was at deadly strife?

14. What woman by her faith did save her life?

15. Who, a fierce foe, did in a monarch find,
But in that monarch's son a friend most kind?

TRUE OR FALSE?

1. In ancient Babylon, the Bible says gold and silver were as plentiful as stones.

2. Rome, for its beauty, was once known as "the glory of kingdoms."

3. At Nob, King David ate the holy bread.

4. Upon Mount Gerazim Israel was cursed for disobedience.

5. Damascus is believed to be the oldest city in the world.

6. On Mount Tabor King Josiah was killed in battle.

7. On Mount Sinai a king commanded a whole nation to be gathered.

Q. Where can you find the first soft drink commercial in the Bible?

A. In the Book of "Have-a-Coke" (Hab-a-kkuk).

8. The cave of Makkedah was the hiding place of five kings.

9. The forces of Sisera and Barek once battled in the area around Mount Tabor.

10. Isaiah and Jeremiah offer prophetic accounts of the manner in which Babylon was captured by the Medes and Persians.

MULTIPLE CHOICE

1. **As Jesus walked to the cross, he warned the 'Daughters of Jerusalem' that they would say this to the mountains:**
   A. Run from us
   B. Rise for us
   C. Fall on us
   D. Protect us
   E. You can't touch this

2. **In the battle of the Amalekites and Israelites what did Moses do on the hill top?**

Q. Where is the first tennis match mentioned in the Bible?

A. When Joseph served in Pharaoh's court.

A. Did a good luck dance
B. Waved them on
C. Held up his hands
D. Prayed
E. Sounded his trumpet

HOW ABOUT THAT!

Some biblical scholars believe that Aramaic did not contain an easy way to say "many things" and used a term which has come down to us as 40. This means that when the Bible—in many places—refers to "40 days," it may mean "many days."

3. Luke quotes a prophecy concerning John the Baptist in which every mountain will be:
A. A high place
B. Green
C. Exalted
D. Made low
E. Climbed

4. Who inherited Shechem in Mount Ephraim?
A. Merarites
B. Children of Aaron
C. Kohathites
D. Gershomites
E. The Grateful Dead

5. **Who dwelt in Mount Seir?**
   A. Esau
   B. Jacob
   C. Lot
   D. Ishmael
   E. Bilbo Baggins

6. **What is remembered at hill Mizar?**
   A. A successful battle
   B. God
   C. Happiness

D. The Alamo
E. The plague of locusts

7. **Jesus was on this mount when he delivered a famous prophecy about the times of the end:**
A. Mount of Olives
B. Mount Sinai
C. Mount Hermon
D. Mount Zion
E. Mount End of the World

8. **As the mountains surround Jerusalem, so the Lord surrounds ____________.**
A. His enemies
B. His people
C. The land
D. The earth
E. The North Pole

9. **What Mount is a Sabbath day's journey from Jerusalem?**
A. Mount Zion
B. Mount Moriah
C. Mount Olivet

Q. Where is the theater mentioned in the Bible?

A. Where Joseph left the family circle and went into the pit.

D. Mount Horeb
E. Mount Olympus

10. Where did Gideon have his army prior to confronting the Midianites?
A. Mount Gilead
B. Mount Tabor
C. Mount Gerizim
D. Mount Gilboa
E. Mount St. Helens

ANSWERS p. 217

SHORT ANSWER

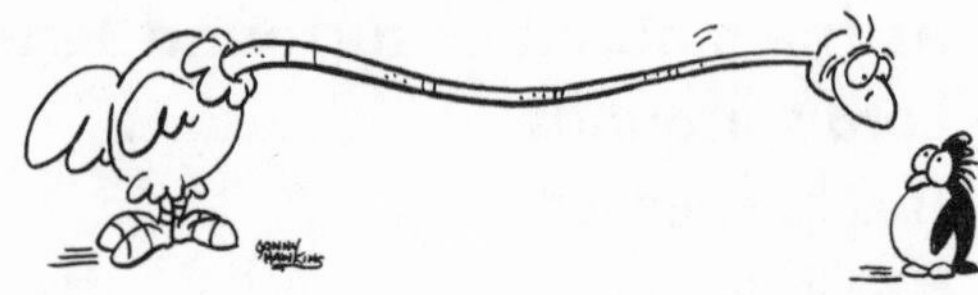

1. Where does the LORD teach us, "In returning and rest you shall be saved; / In quietness and confidence shall be your strength"? ________________

2. Where are we asked, "How can a man be righteous before God?" and told, "If one wished to contend with Him, / He could not answer Him one time out of a thousand." ________________________

Q. If Goliath is resurrected, would you like to tell him the joke about David and Goliath?

A. No, he already fell for it once.

3. Can you identify the source of the following passage:

"Your ears shall hear a word behind you, saying,
'This is the way, walk in it,'
Whenever you turn to the right hand
Or whenever you turn to the left."

____

HOW ABOUT THAT!

There are eight different sizes of champagne bottles, and the largest is called a Nebuchadnezzar—after the biblical king who put Daniel's three friends into the fiery furnace.

4. Who said, "For we were born yesterday, and know nothing," and where is it found? ______________

____

5. Can you locate the statement, "Yet the righteous will hold to his way, And he who has clean hands will be stronger and stronger."? ______________

6. Where is a king spoken of as "The breath of our nostrils"? ______________________

7. Who first employed that powerful simile, "Like an antelope in a net"? ______________________

8. Christ on two occasions quoted the words, "I desire mercy and not sacrifice." Where are they in the Old Testament? ______________________

9. Who said, "No doubt but you are the people, and wisdom shall die with you."? ______________

10. Where do we hear this wise advice:

"The end of a thing is better than its beginning;
The patient in spirit is better than the proud in spirit.
Do not hasten in your spirit to be angry,
For anger rests in the bosom of fools."

____

11. Where does it say, "Let us eat and drink, for tomorrow we die"? ______________

HOW ABOUT THAT!

Only three angels are mentioned by name in the Bible: Gabriel, Michael, and Lucifer.

12. Locate the familiar quotation about the hardening tendency of habitual sinning, "Can the Ethiopian change his skin, or the leopard its spots?"

____

13. Where is the warning against ignoring corrections? "He who is often rebuked, and hardens his neck, will suddenly be destroyed, and that without remedy."

____

14. Where is this verse that declares our dependence on God rather than on ourselves: "Not by might nor by power, but by my Spirit, says the LORD,"

____

15. Where does this warning against lying occur? "You shall not circulate a false report. Do not put your hand with the wicked to be an unrighteous witness." ______________________________

16. Where is it stated, "The LORD saw that the wickedness of man was great in the earth, and that every intent of the thoughts of his heart was only evil continually."? ______________________________

Q. Was Noah the first one out of the Ark?

A. No, he came forth out of the ark.

17. Where does God promise, "I will give your life to you as a prize in all places, wherever you go"?

____

18. Where does it teach, "He who rules his spirit is greater than he who takes a city."? _______________

19. Can you find the location of, "Shall not the Judge of all the earth do right?" _______________

20. Where are we asked, "Shall we accept good from God and shall we not receive adversity?" _______________

ANSWERS TO: WHERE?

MULTIPLE CHOICE

# ANSWER	REFERENCE
1. c.	Psalm 114:4
2. b.	Joel 3:17
3. d.	Genesis 8:4
4. a.	2 Chronicles 3:1
5. c.	Judges 4:7
6. d.	Exodus 31:18
7. a.	Deuteronomy 11:29
8. d.	Deuteronomy 34:1–7
9. c.	Joshua 8:30
10. b.	Deuteronomy 3:9

FILL IN THE BLANKS

# ANSWER	REFERENCE
1. Bethlehem	
2. Philippi	Acts 16:12, 13

# ANSWER	REFERENCE
3. Jordan	
4. Euphrates	Deuteronomy 1:7
5. Kadesh-barnea	Numbers 13:26
6. Midian	Exodus 2:15
7. Patmos	Revelation 1:9
8. Tekoa	Amos 1:1
9. Ramah	1 Samuel 7:17
10. Tarshish; Joppa	Jonah 1:3

BIBLE MATH

# ANSWER				
1. Jesus' temptations + 2	=	5	=	E
Days Lazarus was in tomb ÷ 2	=	2	=	B
Sons of Rachel – 1	=	1	=	A
Elders in Revelation ÷ 2	=	12	=	L
2. Church letters in Revelation – 5	=	2	=	B
Lepers who didn't thank Jesus + 3	=	12	=	L
Chapters in Lamentations	=	5	=	E

BIBLE MATH—cont'd

#	ANSWER				
	Horns of the Beast + 9	=	19	=	S
	Verses in Philemon – 6	=	19	=	S
	Commandments – 1	=	9	=	I
	Ears of corn in Pharaoh's dream	=	14	=	N
	Jesse's sons – 1	=	7	=	G
3.	Steps of Solomon's throne + 1	=	7	=	G
	Psalms ÷ 30	=	5	=	E
	Cities of Refuge × 3	=	18	=	R
	Tribes of Israel – 3	=	9	=	I
	New Testament Books – 1	=	26	=	Z
	Job's friends × 3	=	9	=	I
	Abijah's wives – 1	=	13	=	M
4.	Lamech's wives + 1	=	3	=	C
	Years in wilderness – 19	=	21	=	U
	Years Aeneas was bedridden + 10	=	18	=	R
	Silver paid for Joseph – 1	=	19	=	S
	Loaves Jesus used to feed 5000	=	5	=	E
	Horns of the beast + 9	=	19	=	S

ANSWER

Before they entered the Promised Land they had to pass between E B A L the Mount of B L E S S I N G and G E R I Z I M the Mount of C U R S E S.

TRUE OR FALSE?

#	ANSWER	REFERENCE
1.	True	Joshua 6
2.	False; Armageddon	Revelation 16:16
3.	False; Cana	John 2
4.	True	Acts 11:26
5.	False; A tower	Genesis 11:9
6.	False; Megiddo	2 Chronicles 35:22
7.	False; Dothan	Genesis 37:12–28
8.	True	Genesis 32:3; 36:8
9.	False; Gaza	Judges 16:23–31
10.	False; A lame man	Acts 3:1–10

CROSSWORD PUZZLE

1 J	O	P	2 P	A										3 T		
E			A			4 D	5 A	L	6 M	A	N	U	T	H	A	
R			T				N		I					E		7 T
I			8 M	I	L	E	T	U	S					S		A
C			O				I		S					S		R
H			S			9 C	O	R	I	N	T	H	I	A	N	S
O		10 A					C		O					L		U
		E		11 B	E	T	H	A	N	Y		12 T	R	O	A	S
13 C	A	N	A						A					N		
Y		E		14 C	A	E	S	A	R	E	A			I		
P		A							I					C		
R		S						15 B	E	T	16 H	P	H	A	G	17 E
U									S		E					G
18 S	E	L	E	U	C	I	19 A				R		20 N			Y
							S				M		A			P
21 P	H	I	L	I	P	P	I				22 O	L	I	V	E	T
							23 A	E	N	O	N		N			

SHORT ANSWER

# ANSWER	REFERENCE
1. Zoar	Genesis 19:23
2. Garden of Eden	Genesis 3:8
3. Nineveh	Jonah 3:4

#	ANSWER	REFERENCE
4.	Jerusalem	2 Kings 21:13
5.	Jericho	2 Chronicles 28:15
6.	Bethlehem	Genesis 35:19, 20
7.	Babylon	Isaiah 13:19, 20; Jeremiah 25:12
8.	From the river of Egypt to the Euphrates	Genesis 15:18
9.	Solomon's navy at Ezion-geber on the Red Sea	1 Kings 9:26
10.	Gibeon	Joshua 9:3, 15

WORD SCRAMBLE

#	ANSWER
1.	Capernaum
2.	Bethsaida
3.	Magdala
4.	Nazareth
5.	Bethany
6.	Jerusalem
7.	Emmaus
8.	Cana
9.	Korazin
10.	Nain

WORD SCRAMBLE—cont'd

#	ANSWER
11.	Bethlehem
12.	Gadara

BIBLE JEOPARDY

#	ANSWER
1.	Where is Jericho?
2.	Where is Armageddon?
3.	Where is Cana?
4.	Where is Antioch?
5.	Where is Babel?
6.	Where is Berea?
7.	Where is Dothan?
8.	Where is Edom?
9.	Where is Gaza?
10.	Where is the Beautiful Gate?

MATCHING

#	ANSWER	REFERENCE
1.	a.	Genesis 2:3
2.	g.	Genesis 8:4

#	ANSWER	REFERENCE
3.	e.	Genesis 29:4–5
4.	f.	Psalm 68:15
5.	i.	1 Kings 18:20–40
6.	j.	
7.	d.	Deuteronomy 32:49, 50; 34:6
8.	b.	1 Chronicles 21:15—22:1
9.	h.	Exodus 19:3, 20
10.	c.	1 Kings 8:1; 1 Chronicles 11:5; 2 Chronicles 5:2

WORD FIND

After finding the names of Bible places, the letters left over spell out the puzzle's message.

(G)	(E)	(N)	(A)	(A)	(N)	(A)	(C)
(I)	(N)	(G)	(M)	(Z)	S	I	(N)
(L)	(O)	(E)	(Y)	(O)	(A)	(E)	(N)
(E)	(M)	(D)	N	(P)	(D)	(G)	(E)
(A)	(M)	(O)	A	(E)	(T)	(O)	(H)
(D)	(A)	(M)	(A)	(S)	(C)	(U)	(S)
(L)	(E)	(B)	(A)	(B)	(R)	I	(O)
(J)	(E)	(R)	(I)	(C)	(H)	(O)	(G)

Ammon	Eden
Edom	Babel
Canaan	Damascus
Egypt	Gaza
Gilead	Goshen
Jericho	Moab
Sodom	Ur

Where did Moses receive the Ten Commandments?

On Mount S I N A I.

ENIGMA NO. 1

#	ANSWER	REFERENCE
	THE GOOD SHEPHERD.	
1.	**T**-abitha	Acts 9:36–39
2.	**H**-agar	Genesis 21:14
3.	**E**-zekiel	Ezekiel 1:1
4.	**G**-ehazi	2 Kings 5:25
5.	**O**-reb	Judges 7:25
6.	**O**-badiah	1 Kings 18:5
7.	**D**-aniel	Daniel 6:23
8.	**S**-amson	Judges 15:15
9.	**H**-ezekiah	2 Kings 20:5
10.	**E**-lah	1 Samuel 17:2, 51
11.	**P**-eter	Luke 22:61, 62
12.	**H**-oreb	Exodus 3:1
13.	**E**-sau	Genesis 27:41
14.	**R**-ahab	Hebrews 11:31
15.	**D**-avid	1 Samuel 19:1, 2

TRUE OR FALSE?

#	ANSWER	REFERENCE
1.	False; In Jerusalem during the reign of Solomon	1 King 10:25–27; 2 Chronicles 1:15

#	ANSWER	REFERENCE
2.	False; Babylon	Isaiah 13:19
3.	True	1 Samuel 21:1, 6
4.	False; Mount Ebal	Deuteronomy 27:13
5.	True	Genesis 14:15
6.	True	2 Kings 23:29
7.	False; Mount Carmel by King Ahab	1 Kings 18:20
8.	True	Joshua 10:16
9.	True	Judges 4:15
10.	True	Isaiah 13:l,22; 14:22; Jeremiah 1

MULTIPLE CHOICE

#	ANSWER	REFERENCE
1.	c.	Luke 23:28–30
2.	c.	Exodus 17:8–16
3.	d.	Luke 3:4–5
4.	c.	Joshua 21:21
5.	a.	Genesis 36:8
6.	b.	Psalm 42:6
7.	a.	Mark 13:3

MULTIPLE CHOICE—cont'd

#	ANSWER	REFERENCE
8.	b.	Psalm 125:2
9.	c.	Acts 1:12
10.	a.	Judges 7:1–3

SHORT ANSWER

#	ANSWER
1.	Isaiah 30:15
2.	Job 9:2, 3
3.	Isaiah 30:21
4.	Bildad the Shuhite, Job 8:9
5.	Job 17:9
6.	Lamentations 4:20
7.	Isaiah, Isaiah 51:20
8.	Hosea 6:6
9.	Job, Job 12:2
10.	Ecclesiastes 7:8–9
11.	Isaiah 22:13
12.	Jeremiah 13:23
13.	Proverbs 29:1
14.	Zechariah 4:6, 10

#	ANSWER
15.	Exodus 23:1
16.	Genesis 6:5; 8:21
17.	Jeremiah 45:5
18.	Proverbs 16:32
19.	Genesis 18:25
20.	Job 2:10

Why?

MULTIPLE CHOICE

1. **Abraham was prepared to kill his only son Isaac. Why?**
   - **A.** Isaac had wrecked the camel.
   - **B.** Abraham's other son, Ishmael, told lies about Isaac.
   - **C.** There was not enough food to feed him.
   - **D.** God had commanded it.

2. **In a single word, why did Cain kill Abel?**
   - **A.** Inheritance
   - **B.** Jealousy
   - **C.** Revenge
   - **D.** Plastics

ANSWERS p. 251

3. **Why did Moses have his brother speak for him?**
   - **A.** Laryngitis
   - **B.** He could also do some neat sound effects.
   - **C.** Exhaustion
   - **D.** A lack of eloquence

4. **Why did Saul seek the services of the witch of Endor?**
   - **A.** To obtain a love potion
   - **B.** The Ewoks told him to.
   - **C.** To communicate with the spirit of his deceased mentor Samuel
   - **D.** To assure victory in battle

5. **Why did David refuse to use the armor offered to him before his battle with Goliath?**
   A. It was untested.
   B. It was the wrong color.
   C. It was too large.
   D. It was obsolete.

6. **Why did God allow enemies to conquer both the Northern and Southern kingdoms?**
   A. Because they refused to draft young men into the military
   B. Because of their idolatry and injustice
   C. Because he was paying attention to other nations
   D. Because they needed to get out of gambling debt

7. **Why did Haman want a gallows constructed?**
   A. To provide employment for his townspeople
   B. As a warning to thieves
   C. To hang Mordecai
   D. To auction off slaves

8. **Why was the king astounded when he looked into the fiery furnace?**
   A. His gold ore refused to melt.
   B. His marshmallows wouldn't roast.
   C. The fire did not go out even though the fuel was exhausted.
   D. He saw a fourth figure like the Son of Man.

9. **Why is Micah considered a minor prophet?**
   A. His book of prophecy is very short.
   B. He was very short.

C. His temper was very short.
D. His prophecies were in a sad key.

10. **According to Psalm 8, what is man?**
A. A fatter, wingless angel
B. Only an animal
C. A little lower than the angels
D. Superior to everything but God

FILL IN THE BLANKS

1. We find stories of Moses in ______________.

2. Two books of the Bible, ______________ and ______________, do not mention the name of God.

3. Two books in the New Testament, ______________ and ______________, were probably written by a doctor.

4. ______________ is called "the drama" of the Bible.

5. ______________ is full of wise sayings.

6. The Ten Commandants are found in ______________ and ______________.

7. The Lord's Prayer is found in ______________.

8. ______________ is the Shepherd Psalm.

9. We find stories of the early Christian church in ______________.

10. The Beatitudes are found in ______________.

11. The names of the Gospels are ______________, ______________, ______________, and ______________.

12. The word "Gospel" means ____________.

13. The Gospel according to ____________ contains the most parables.

WORD BANK

Exodus 20	Luke	Good News
Exodus	Mark	Psalm 23
Matthew 5	Proverbs	Song of Solomon
Deuteronomy 5	Esther	Acts
Matthew 6	Acts	Matthew
Luke 11	John	Luke	Job

BIBLE MATH

ANSWERS p. 252

Daniel wasn't the only servant of God tested by Nebuchadnezzer. Fill in the puzzle below and find out who else trusted in God for their rescue. Each answer is a number that matches a letter of the alphabet (A=1, B=2, C=3 . . .). Put that letter in the blank next to the number and then in the quote at the bottom to find the missing words. The first one is done for you.

1st Word

Commandments + 9 = 19 = S

Years Aeneas was bedridden = ___ = ___

Jesus' temptations – 2 = ___ = ___

Trinity + 1 = ___ = ___

Wings of "Living Creatures + 1 = ___ = ___

Chapters in Ruth – 3 = ___ = ___

Spies hidden by Rahab + 1 = ___ = ___

Days Joshua circled Jericho + 1 = ___ = ___

2nd Word

Sons of Jacob + 1 = ___ = ___

Lepers healed by Jesus ÷ 2 = ___ = ___

Years Jacob worked for Rachel = ___ = ___

Gospels × 2 = ___ = ___

Sons of Noah ÷ 3 = ___ = ___

People in Eden + 1 = ___ = ___

Jairus' daughter's age – 4 = ___ = ___

3rd Word

Cities of Refuge – 5 = ___ = ___

Silver coins in Luke 15 ÷ 5 = ___ = ___

Sons of Noah + 2 = ___ = ___

Chariots in Zechariah 6 = ___ = ___

Springs at Elim + 2 = ___ = ___

Chapters in James = ___ = ___

Horsemen in Revelation + 3 = ___ = ___

Verses in Jude – 10 = ___ = ___

4th Word

Living Creatures in Ezekiel + 15 = ___ = ___

Days Lazarus was in tomb + 1 = ___ = ___

Plagues on Egypt + 8 = ___ = ___

Jesus' days in desert – 18 = ___ = ___

Chapters in Habakkuk – 2 = ___ = ___

Jesse's sons + 6 = ___ = ___

Noah's days of rain ÷ 2 = ___ = ___

New Testament books – 7 = ___ = ___

S _ _ _ _ _ _ _ _ _, _ _ _ _ _ _ _ _ _ _,

and _ _ _ _ _ _ _ _ _ _.

_ _ _ _ _ _ _ _ _ _ of the Most High God.

TRUE OR FALSE

1. The fierce "bulls of Bashan" are only mentioned in the book of Revelation.

2. The industriousness of the ant is lauded in Proverbs.

3. The star of Bethlehem is the only star mentioned in the New Testament.

4. Daniel and his friends obtained vegetables and water to take the place of the king's wine, meat, and delicacies.

5. Gold, frankincense, and myrrh were the three gifts the wise men offered to the infant Jesus.

6. David used a scarlet thread placed in his window to signal his men.

HOW ABOUT THAT!

The first book printed with movable metal type was the Gutenberg Bible, printed by Johannes Gutenberg, before August 15, 1456, in Mainz, Germany.

7. Noah's ark was 450 feet long, 75 feet wide, and 45 feet high.

8. Noah and his wife were the only human beings on the ark.

9. In addition to the pairs of every animal and bird, Noah took seven of every clean animal, male and female.

10. A dove was the only bird sent forth from the ark by Noah.

CROSSWORD PUZZLE

Across

1. Ephraim's oldest son and the founder of a tribal family (Numbers 26:36)
3. Belonging to the original home of the Syrians (Amos 9:7)

4. Ruler
6. At the very center
8. Exclamation of derision
9. Total
11. Author of most of the New Testament letters
12. Person without living parents
13. Thief
15. Abbreviation of the name of the prophet who declared, "What the Lord requires of you . . ."
17. Where Jesus performed his first miracle
18. The epitome of suffering
20. Glowing embers
21. An abbreviation for a major prophet
23. Clans

Down

1. Priest in time of Samuel
2. Correct
4. Jesus was betrayed with this
5. Snare
6. Lazarus would have been happy with them.
7. King of the Jews in Latin (abbrev.)
8. So be it
10. The mother of Jesus
13. Most commonly used hand (abbrev.)
14. Name in Genesis 46:21.
15. A son of Mushi (1 Chronicles 23:23)

16. Body of believers
19. Unclean flying creature
20. A Hebrew dry measure
22. The promised Comforter (abbrev.)

SHORT ANSWER

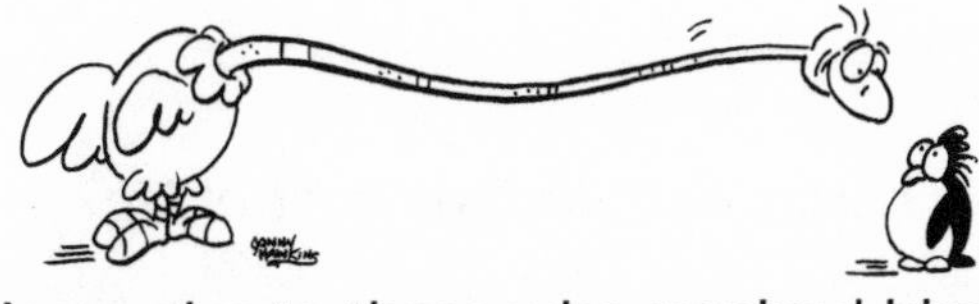

1. What did Jesus give to those who received him?

   ____

   How were they born? ______________________________

2. What did John say when he saw Jesus coming toward him? ______________________________

   ____

3. How much did God love the world? ______________________________

   ____

4. How is the "water" given by Jesus different from ordinary water? ______________________________

   ____

5. How should we worship God? ______________________________

6. When Jesus gave instructions on worship, how did he describe God? ______________________________

   ____

7. Is eternal life found in searching the Scriptures?

____

8. When Jesus said, "I am the bread of life," what did he promise? _______________

____

9. How do we find the light of life? _______________

____

10. Who are the true disciples of Jesus? _______________

____

11. What shall make us free? _______________

12. How is the coming of Jesus different than coming of the thief? _______________

13. Who shall never die? _______________

14. What was the "new commandment" that Jesus gave his disciples? _______________

____

15. Why should we not be troubled? What does Jesus promise to those who believe in God and also in him?

____

16. How does one come to the Father? _______________

____

17. Who bears much fruit? ______________________

18. Though we find tribulation in the world, why should we be cheerful? ______________________

19. What was Thomas' confession and what did Jesus say about it? ______________________

20. Why did the author of the fourth gospel say that it had been written? ______________________

WORD SCRAMBLE

Who were the twelve tribes of Israel? Unscramble the letters below to find out.

1. MEJNINBA _ _ _ _ _ _ _ _
2. LIVE _ _ _ _
3. ADUHJ _ _ _ _ _
4. HARSHE _ _ _ _ _ _
5. ATHILAPN _ _ _ _ _ _ _ _
6. AND _ _ _
7. ONESMI _ _ _ _ _ _
8. AGD _ _ _
9. UNBREE _ _ _ _ _ _

ANSWERS p. 261

10. NEULBZU _ _ _ _ _ _ _ _

11. CHSAIRSA _ _ _ _ _ _ _ _

12. ESOPHJ _ _ _ _ _ _ _

BIBLE JEOPARDY

$100	$200	$300	$400	DAILY DOUBLE	$500	$600	$700	$800	$900

Here are the answers. Do you know the questions?

1. Because of Queen Maachah's idolatry, this happened. (1 Kings 15:13)

2. Because Moses' face shone after he had been in the presence of the LORD, he did this. (Exodus 34:33)

3. Because Moses witnessed Aaron and the Israelites worshipping an idol, he did this in anger. (Exodus 32:16–19)

4. To symbolize the coming conquest of the middle east by the Babylonian king Nebuchadnezzar, Jeremiah did this. (Jeremiah 27:2)

5. Because Moses murdered an Egyptian who had been beating a Hebrew. (Exodus 2:11–15)

6. Because Nadab and Abihu, the sons of Aaron, offered "profane fire." (Leviticus 10:1–2)

7. Lest he become overly content and deny the Lord, Agur, the son of Jakeh, did this. (Proverbs 30:7–9)

8. Because he wanted to learn with the priests and scribes in his father's house. (Luke 2:41–50)

9. Because he "was very much afraid of Achish the king of Gath," David did this. (1 Samuel 21:12)

10. Because they complained that the residents of the Promised Land would overcome them in battle and stating that they preferred returning to Egypt. (Numbers 14:34)

MATCHING

Each of the following paragraphs is the final verse of one of the books of the Bible listed in the right column. Can you match the verse with the book?

1. Unless You have utterly rejected us, And are very angry with us!	a. Titus
2. This salutation by my own hand—Paul. Remember my chains. Grace be with you. Amen.	b. Ruth
3. They will take up serpents; and if they drink anything deadly, it will by no means hurt them; they will lay hands on the sick, and they will recover.	c. Revelation

4. Then Paul dwelt two whole years in his own rented house, and received all who came to him, preaching the kingdom of God and teaching the things which concern the Lord Jesus Christ with all confidence, no one forbidding him.	d. Matthew
5. The grace of our Lord Jesus Christ be with you all. Amen.	e. Mark
6. So Joseph died, being one hundred and ten years old; and they embalmed him, and he was put in a coffin in Egypt.	f. Malachi
7. Obed begot Jesse, and Jesse begot David.	g. Luke
8. Little children, keep yourselves from idols. Amen.	h. Lamentations
9. In those days there was no king in Israel; everyone did what was right in his own eyes.	i. Judges
10. Grace be with you all. Amen.	j. Jeremiah
11. Go therefore and make disciples of all the nations, baptizing them in the name of the Father and of the Son and of the Holy Spirit, teaching them to observe all things that I have commanded you; and lo, I am with	

you always, even to the end of the age. Amen.	k. Hebrews
12. For the cloud of the LORD *was* above the tabernacle by day, and fire was over it by night, in the sight of all the house of Israel, throughout all their journeys.	l. Genesis
13. For he served Baal and worshiped him, and provoked the LORD God of Israel to anger, according to all that his father had done.	m. Galatians
14. For God will bring every work into judgment, Including every secret thing, Whether good or evil.	n. Ezekiel
15. But you, go your way till the end; for you shall rest, and will arise to your inheritance at the end of the days.	o. Exodus
16. Brethren, the grace of our Lord Jesus Christ be with your spirit. Amen.	p. Ecclesiastes
17. And they worshiped Him, and returned to Jerusalem with great joy, and were continually in the temple praising and blessing God. Amen.	q. Deuteronomy

18. And he will turn The hearts of the fathers to the children, And the hearts of the children To their fathers, Lest I come and strike the earth with a curse.

r. Daniel

19. and by all that mighty power and all the great terror which Moses performed in the sight of all Israel.

s. Colossians

20. And as for his provisions, there was a regular ration given him by the king of Babylon, a portion for each day until the day of his death, all the days of his life.

t. Acts

ANSWERS p. 262

21. All who are with me greet you. Greet those who love us in the faith. Grace be with you all. Amen.

u. 1 Kings

22. All the way around shall be eighteen thousand cubits; and the name of the city from that day shall be: THE LORD IS THERE.

v. 1 John

WORD FIND

Find each of the words listed below in the puzzle. They read in a straight line vertically, horizontally, diagonally (and backwards, of course). Circle each letter of each word. The letters left over spell out the puzzle message (KJV).

S	T	R	O	T	C	E	L	H
E	L	B	A	R	A	P	P	L
S	C	R	I	P	T	U	R	E
R	Y	W	B	O	E	Y	A	P
E	P	O	R	L	C	D	Y	S
V	O	S	B	L	H	U	E	O
K	D	I	A	I	I	T	R	G
S	B	S	A	L	S	S	L	A
M	S	Y	L	I	M	O	H	P

Book	Bible
Catechism	Class
Gospel	Homily
Lector	Parable
Prayer	Psalm
Scripture	Study
Verses	

___ ___ ___   ___ ___ ___ ___   ___ ___   ___

___ ___ ___ ___.

ENIGMA NO. 1

What is Christian worship?
You shall quickly know,
When you solve the queries
Following here below.

1. Name the fifth disciple,
   Of Bethsaida he,
   Jesus found, and called him,
   "Friend, follow me!"

2. How shall we take warning,
Learning from Lot's wife,
Who, though saved from Sodom,
Turned and lost her life?

3. With the traitor's silver,
When this field was bought,
There the doom he suffered,
Of the deeds he wrought.

4. Paul once found at Corinth,
Lately come from where?
Two good souls when Caesar,
Drove all Jews from there.

5. Early in the morning,
With the Marys came,
One, to look for Jesus,
Mark recites her name.

6. Jacob's father's father—
Tell his worthy name.
In the line of David,
You shall find the same.

ANSWERS
p. 264

To Solve:
First the initial letters,
Next the finals take;
Then, with holy incense
These sweet offerings make
This to tell God's mercies,
That to seek his face,
Through the blood of sprinkling,
At the throne of grace.

Q. How do we know Cain took a nap when he left Eden?

A. He went to the land of Nod.

MATCHING

Can you straighten these Q & As out by placing the correct answer with its proper question? Warning: one of the answers is fine right where it is.

1. How does the Bible describe the fruitfulness of Canaan?	a. *In four Bible passages.*
2. What did the Jews place in the compartments of their phylacteries?	b. *About three pecks, five quarts.*
3. In picturing the coming Christ, what did John the Baptist say would be in his hand?	c. *A tiny grain of mustard seed.*
4. By what was Jonah swallowed up?	d. *"A land flowing with milk and honey."*
5. To what did Christ compare his kingdom in its little beginnings?	e. *Rats.*
6. Why did the sun and moon stand still at the command of Joshua?	f. *That the Israelites might avenge themselves on their enemies.*
7. About how large was an ephah?	g. *A winnowing fork.*

8. What became of the thirty pieces of silver for which Judas betrayed Christ?

9. Golden images of what animals were returned by the plague-stricken Philistines together with the Ark of the Covenant?

10. As Gideon's three hundred men attacked the Midianites, what means did they use to produce terror?

h. *A great fish.*

i. *They blew their trumpets, smashed their pitchers, and waved the torches which had been concealed by the pitchers.*

j. *He threw thirty pieces of silver back at the chief priests and elders, who used them to buy the potter's field to bury strangers in.*

FILL IN THE BLANKS

1. "Seek the LORD while He may be found,
   Call upon Him while He is near.
   Let the wicked forsake his way,
   And the unrighteous man his thoughts;
   Let him return to the LORD,

And He will have mercy on him;

And to our God,

For He will abundantly ____________."

(Isaiah 55:6, 7)

2. "'Yet from the days of your fathers

You have gone away from My ordinances

And have not kept *them.*

____________ to Me, and I will ______________ to you,'

Says the LORD of hosts.

But you said,

'In what way shall we ______________?'"

(Malachi 3:7)

3. "But to you who fear My name

The Sun of ____________________ shall arise

With healing in His wings;

Q. Why was Adam a famous runner?

A. Because he was first in the human race.

And you shall go out
And grow fat like stall-fed calves."
(Malachi 4:2)

4. "You shall be called by a new ________________,
Which the mouth of the LORD will ____________."
(Isaiah 62:19)

5. "For the LORD will comfort Zion,
He will comfort all her waste places;
He will make her wilderness like Eden,
And her desert like the garden of the LORD;
Joy and gladness will be found in it,
Thanksgiving and the voice of ______________."
(Isaiah 51:3)

ANSWERS p. 268

6. "I will bring the blind by a way they did not know;
I will lead them in paths they have not known.
I will make darkness light before them,
And crooked places straight.
These things I will do for them,
And not ______________ them."
(Isaiah 42:16)

WORD BANK

melody	name	Righteousness
return	pardon	forsake
Return	name	return

MATCHING

1. Why have I found favor in your eyes, that you should take notice of me, since I am a foreigner?	a. Ecclesiastes 7:10
2. Why do you transgress the commandments of the Lord, so that you cannot prosper? Because you have forsaken the Lord, He also has forsaken you.	b. Genesis 31:27
3. Why then do you lay a snare for my life, to cause me to die?	c. 1 Samuel 28:9
4. Why should I be bereaved also of you both in one day?	d. 2 Samuel 7:7
5. Why have you not built Me a house of cedar?	e. 2 Chronicles 24:20

6. Why did I come forth from the womb to see labor and sorrow?	f. Psalm 74:1
7. Why did you flee away secretly, and steal away from me, and not tell me; for I might have sent you away with joy and songs, with timbrel and harp?	g. Ruth 2:10

HOW ABOUT THAT!

There are more predictions in the Bible than there are commands. The number of predictions is 8,000, while the number of commands is 6,468.

8. Why do you gad about so much to change your way?	h. Numbers 20:4
9. Why does Your anger smoke against the sheep of Your pasture?	i. Job 27:1
10. Why have you brought up the assembly of the	j. Jeremiah 20:18

Lord into this wilderness, that we and our animals should die here?

11.	Why then do you behave with complete nonsense?	k.	Genesis 27:45
12.	Why were the former days better than these?	l.	Jeremiah 2:36

ANSWERS TO: WHY?

MULTIPLE CHOICE

#	ANSWER	REFERENCE
1.	d.	Genesis 22:1–19
2.	b.	1 John 3:10–12
3.	d.	Exodus 4:10–17
4.	c.	1 Samuel 28:7–25
5.	a.	1 Samuel 17:38–39
6.	b.	2 Kings 17:1–20
7.	c.	Esther 5:14
8.	d.	Daniel 3:23–25
9.	a.	
10.	c.	Psalm 8:5

FILL IN THE BLANKS

#	ANSWER
1.	Exodus
2.	Esther and Song of Solomon
3.	Luke and Acts
4.	Job
5.	Proverbs

FILL IN THE BLANKS—cont'd

#	ANSWER
6.	Exodus 20 and Deuteronomy 5
7.	Matthew 6 and Luke 11
8.	Psalm 23
9.	Acts
10.	Matthew 5
11.	Matthew, Mark, Luke and John
12.	Good News
13.	Luke

BIBLE MATH

#	ANSWER		
1.	Commandments + 9	= 19	= S
	Years Aeneas was bedridden	= 8	= H
	Jesus' temptations – 2	= 1	= A
	Trinity + 1	= 4	= D
	Wings of "Living Creatures + 1	= 18	= R
	Chapters in Ruth – 3	= 1	= A
	Spies hidden by Rahab + 1	= 3	= C
	Days Joshua circled Jericho + 1	= 8	= H

#	ANSWER			
2.	Sons of Jacob + 1	= 13	=	M
	Lepers healed by Jesus ÷ 2	= 5	=	E
	Years Jacob worked for Rachel	= 19	=	S
	Gospels × 2	= 8	=	H
	Sons of Noah ÷ 3	= 1	=	A
	People in Eden + 1	= 3	=	C
	Jairus' daughter's age – 4	= 8	=	H
3.	Cities of Refuge – 5	= 1	=	A
	Silver coins in Luke 15 ÷ 5	= 2	=	B
	Sons of Noah + 2	= 5	=	E
	Chariots in Zechariah 6	= 4	=	D
	Springs at Elim + 2	= 14	=	N
	Chapters in James	= 5	=	E
	Horsemen in Revelation + 3	= 7	=	G
	Verses in Jude – 10	= 15	=	O
4.	Living Creatures in Ezekiel + 15	= 19	=	S
	Days Lazarus was in tomb + 1	= 5	=	E
	Plagues on Egypt + 8	= 18	=	R
	Jesus' days in desert – 18	= 22	=	V
	Chapters in Habakkuk – 2	= 1	=	A

BIBLE MATH—cont'd

#	ANSWER		
	Jesse's sons + 6	= 14	= N
	Noah's days of rain ÷ 2	= 20	= T
	New Testament books – 7	= 9	= S

S H A D R A C H, M E S H A C H,

and A B E D N E G O.

S E R V A N T S of the Most High God.

TRUE OR FALSE

#	ANSWER	REFERENCE
1.	False	Psalm 22:12
2.	True	Proverbs 6:6–8
3.	False	See Acts 7:43, 1 Corinthians 15:41, 2 Peter 1:19, Revelation 2:28, Revelation 8:10–11; Revelation 9:1; Revelation 22:16

#	ANSWER	REFERENCE
4.	True	Daniel 1:12
5.	True	Matthew 2:11
6.	False; A scarlet thread was used as a signal by Rahab, who was preserved in the fall of Jericho by placing it in her window.	Joshua 2:18
7.	True; Taking the cubit at 18 inches	Genesis 6:15
8.	False; Noah, his wife, and their three sons and their wives	Genesis 7:1–7
9.	True	Genesis 7:2
10.	False; A raven was first sent forth by Noah from the ark.	Genesis 8:6, 7

Q. Why was Adam created first?

A. To give him a chance to say something.

CROSSWORD PUZZLE

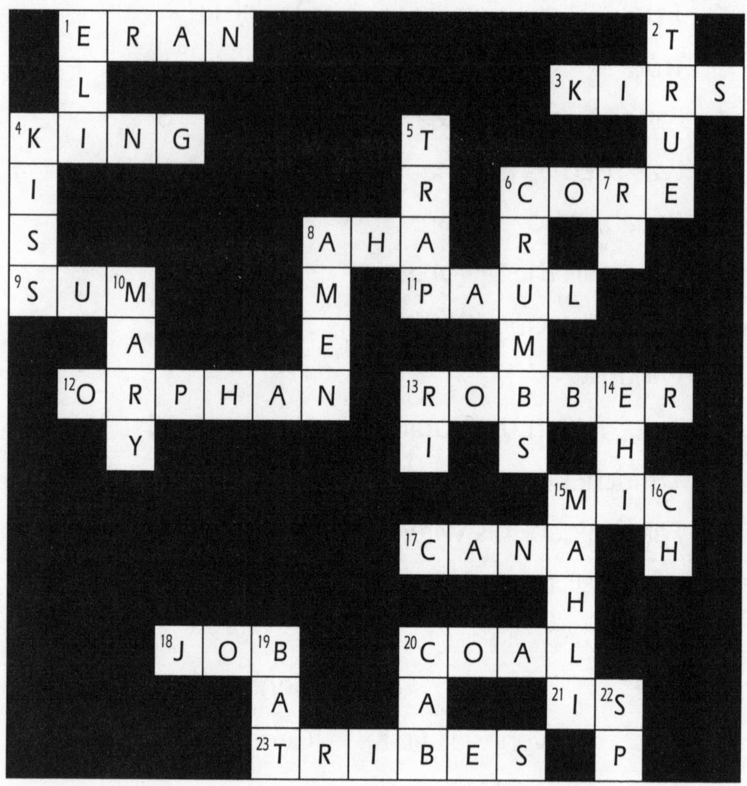

SHORT ANSWER

#	ANSWER	REFERENCE
1.	"But as many as received Him, to them He gave the right to become children of God, to those	John 1:12–13

#	ANSWER	REFERENCE
	who believe in His name: who were born, not of blood, nor of the will of the flesh, nor of the will of man, but of God."	
2.	"Behold! The Lamb of God who takes away the sin of the world!"	John 1:29
3.	"For God so loved the world that He gave His only begotten Son, that whoever believes in Him should not perish but have everlasting life."	John 3:16
4.	". . . but whoever drinks of the water that I shall give him will never thirst. But the water that I shall give him will become in him a fountain of water springing up into everlasting life."	John 4:14
5.	"But the hour is coming, and now is, when the true worshipers will worship the Father in spirit and truth; for the Father is seeking such to worship Him."	John 4:23
6.	"God is Spirit, and those who worship Him must worship in spirit and truth."	John 4:24

SHORT ANSWER—cont'd

#	ANSWER	REFERENCE
7.	"You search the Scriptures, for in them you think you have eternal life; and these are they which testify of Me."	John 5:39
8.	"And Jesus said to them, 'I am the bread of life. He who comes to Me shall never hunger, and he who believes in Me shall never thirst.' "	John 6:35
9.	"Then Jesus spoke to them again, saying, 'I am the light of the world. He who follows Me shall not walk in darkness, but have the light of life.' "	John 8:12
10.	"Then Jesus said to those Jews who believed Him, 'If you abide in My word, you are My disciples indeed.' "	John 8:31
11.	"And you shall know the truth, and the truth shall make you free."	John 8:32
12.	"The thief does not come except to steal, and to kill, and to destroy. I have come that they may	John 10:10

#	ANSWER	REFERENCE
	have life, and that they may have it more abundantly."	
13.	"Jesus said to her, 'I am the resurrection and the life. He who believes in Me, though he may die, he shall live. And whoever lives and believes in Me shall never die. Do you believe this?'"	John 11:25–26
14.	"A new commandment I give to you, that you love one another; as I have loved you, that you also love one another. By this all men will know that you are My disciples, if you have love for one another."	John 13:34–35
15.	"Let not your heart be troubled; you believe in God, believe also in Me. In My Father's house are many mansions; if it were not so, I would have told you. I go to prepare a place for you. And if I go and prepare a place for you, I will come again and receive you to Myself; that where I am, there you may be also."	John 14:1–3

SHORT ANSWER—cont'd

#	ANSWER	REFERENCE
16.	"Jesus said to him, 'I am the way, the truth, and the life. No one comes to the Father except through Me.' "	John 14:6
17.	"I am the vine, you are the branches. He who abides in Me, and I in him, bears much fruit; for without Me you can do nothing. If you abide in Me, and My words abide in you, you will ask what you desire, and it shall be done for you."	John 15:5–7
18.	"These things I have spoken to you, that in Me you may have peace. In the world you will have tribulation; but be of good cheer, I have overcome the world."	John 16:33
19.	"And Thomas answered and said to Him, 'My Lord and my God!' Jesus said to him, 'Thomas, because you have seen Me, you have believed. Blessed are those who have not seen and yet have believed.' "	John 20:28–29

#	ANSWER	REFERENCE
20.	". . . but these are written that you may believe that Jesus is the Christ, the Son of God, and that believing you may have life in His name."	John 20:31

WORD SCRAMBLE

#	ANSWER
1.	Benjamin
2.	Levi
3.	Judah
4.	Asher
5.	Naphtali
6.	Dan
7.	Simeon
8.	Gad
9.	Reuben
10.	Zebulun
11.	Issachar
12.	Joseph

BIBLE JEOPARDY

#	ANSWER
1.	Why was Queen Maachah deprived of her throne by her grandson?
2.	Why did Moses wear a veil?
3.	Why did Moses shatter the Ten Commandments in anger?
4.	Why did Jeremiah put bonds and yokes on his neck?
5.	Why did Moses flee from the land of Egypt?
6.	Why were two men burned to death in the tabernacle?
7.	Why did Agur pray that he might never become rich?
8.	Why did Jesus stay behind at the temple at the age of 12?
9.	Why did David feign to be insane in the presence of an enemy?
10.	Why were the Israelites kept in the wilderness for forty years?

MATCHING

#	ANSWER	REFERENCE
1.	h.	Lamentations 5:22
2.	s.	Colossians 4:18
3.	e.	Mark 16:18

#	ANSWER	REFERENCE
4.	t.	Acts 28:30–31
5.	c.	Revelation 22:21
6.	l.	Genesis 50:26
7.	b.	Ruth 4:22
8.	v.	1 John 5:21
9.	i.	Judges 21:25
10.	k.	Hebrews 13:25
11.	d.	Matthew 28:19–20
12.	o.	Exodus 40:38
13.	u.	1 Kings 22:53
14.	p.	Ecclesiastes 12:14
15.	r.	Daniel 12:13
16.	m.	Galatians 6:18
17.	g.	Luke 24:52–53
18.	f.	Malachi 4:6
19.	q.	Deuteronomy 34:12
20.	j.	Jeremiah 52:34
21.	a.	Titus 3:15
22.	n.	Ezekiel 48:35

Q. Why did Noah punish the chickens?

A. Because they were using fowl language.

WORD FIND

After finding each of the words listed below in the puzzle, the letters left over spell out the puzzle message.

Ⓢ	T	Ⓡ	Ⓞ	Ⓣ	Ⓒ	Ⓔ	Ⓛ	H
Ⓔ	Ⓛ	Ⓑ	Ⓐ	Ⓡ	Ⓐ	Ⓟ	Ⓟ	Ⓛ
Ⓢ	Ⓒ	Ⓡ	Ⓘ	Ⓟ	Ⓣ	Ⓤ	Ⓡ	Ⓔ
Ⓡ	Y	W	Ⓑ	O	Ⓔ	Ⓨ	Ⓐ	Ⓟ
Ⓔ	Ⓟ	Ⓞ	R	Ⓛ	Ⓒ	Ⓓ	Ⓨ	Ⓢ
Ⓥ	Ⓞ	Ⓢ	Ⓑ	Ⓛ	Ⓗ	Ⓤ	Ⓔ	Ⓞ
Ⓚ	D	Ⓘ	Ⓐ	I	Ⓘ	Ⓣ	Ⓡ	Ⓖ
S	Ⓑ	Ⓢ	A	Ⓛ	Ⓢ	Ⓢ	L	Ⓐ
M	Ⓢ	Ⓨ	Ⓛ	Ⓘ	Ⓜ	Ⓞ	Ⓗ	P

Book	Bible
Catechism	Class
Gospel	Homily
Lector	Parable
Prayer	Psalm
Scripture	Study
Verses	

T H Y   W O R D   I S   A
L A M P.

ENIGMA NO. 1

# ANSWER	REFERENCE
Initials—"PRAISE"	Finals—"PRAYER"
1. **P**-hili-**p**	Matthew 10:3; John 1:43–44
2. **R**-emembe-**r**	Luke 17:32
3. **A**-celdam-**a**	Acts 1:18–19
4. **I**-tal-**y**	Acts 18:1–2
5. **S**-alom-**e**	Mark 16:1
6. **E**-leaza-**r**	Matthew 1:15

MATCHING

#	ANSWER	REFERENCE
1.	d.	Exodus 3:17
2.	a.	Exodus 13:2–10, 11–17; Deuteronomy 6:4—9:11:13–21
3.	g.	Matthew 3:12 and Luke 3:17
4.	h.	Jonah 1:17
5.	c.	Mark 4:30
6.	f.	Joshua 10:12–14
7.	b.	Isaiah 5:10
8.	j.	Matthew 27:3–10
9.	e.	1 Samuel 6:4
10.	i.	Judges 7:16–20

FILL IN THE BLANKS

#	ANSWER
1.	pardon
2.	Return, return, return
3.	Righteousness
4.	name, name
5.	melody
6.	forsake

MATCHING

#	ANSWER	REFERENCE
1.	g. "So she fell on her face, bowed down to the ground, and said to him [Boaz], 'Why have I found favor in your eyes, that you should take notice of me, since I am a foreigner?' "	Ruth 2:10
2.	e. "Then the Spirit of God came upon Zechariah the son of Jehoiada the priest, who stood above the people, and said to them, 'Thus says God: 'Why do you transgress the commandments of the Lord, so that you cannot prosper? Because you have forsaken the Lord, He also has forsaken you.' ' "	2 Chronicles 24:20
3.	c. "Then the woman said to him, 'Look, you know what Saul has done, how he has cut off the mediums and the spiritists from the land. Why then do you lay a	1 Samuel 28:9

#	ANSWER	REFERENCE
	snare for my life, to cause me to die?' "	
4. k.	". . . until your brother's anger turns away from you, and he forgets what you have done to him; then I will send and bring you from there. Why should I be bereaved also of you both in one day?"	Genesis 27:45
5. d.	" 'Wherever I have moved about with all the children of Israel, have I ever spoken a word to anyone from the tribes of Israel, whom I commanded to shepherd My people Israel, saying, 'Why have you not built Me a house of cedar?' ' "	2 Samuel 7:7
6. j.	"Why did I come forth from the womb to see labor and sorrow, That my days should be consumed with shame?"	Jeremiah 20:18

MATCHING—cont'd

#	ANSWER	REFERENCE
7.	b. "Why did you flee away secretly, and steal away from me, and not tell me; for I might have sent you away with joy and songs, with timbrel and harp?"	Genesis 31:27
8.	l. "Why do you gad about so much to change your way? Also you shall be ashamed of Egypt as you were ashamed of Assyria."	Jeremiah 2:36
9.	f. "O God, Why have You cast us off forever? Why does Your anger smoke against the sheep of Your pasture?"	Psalm 74:1
10.	h. "Why have you brought up the assembly of the Lord into this wilderness, that we and our animals should die here?"	Numbers 20:4
11.	i. "Surely all of you have seen it; Why then do you behave with complete nonsense?"	Job 27:1

#	ANSWER	REFERENCE
12.	a. "Do not say, 'Why were the former days better than these?' For you do not inquire wisely concerning this."	Ecclesiastes 7:10

How?

MULTIPLE CHOICE

1. **Of what defeated king and prince does the Bible say, "How are the mighty fallen"?**
   A. David and Solomon
   B. Saul and Jonathan
   C. Samson and Goliath
   D. King Tut and Prince Caspian

ANSWERS p. 298

2. **How were the Israelites commanded to treat strangers?**
   A. Love them as themselves.
   B. Kill them as soon as possible.
   C. Treat them as if they didn't know them.
   D. Invite them to dinner.

3. **A boy was once sent to carry to his brothers some loaves and some dried grain. The army to which his brothers belonged gained a great victory in consequence of this visit. What was the name of the boy? How was the victory won?**
   A. Jesus. He summoned legions of angels.
   B. Isaac. He captured a ram for sacrifice.
   C. David. He slew Goliath.
   D. Kevin. He set traps all over the house to catch the two thieves.

4. **How was it that Ahaziah, the youngest son of Jehoram, King of Israel, came to the throne upon the death of his father?**

A. Because his father chose him
B. Because he was the strongest
C. Because he was anointed king by the Prophet Elijah
D. Because a band of raiders had slain all the elder sons

5. **For what purpose did Jeremiah use the image of good and bad figs?**
   A. To illustrate God's dealings with those of the house of Judah who had gone into captivity, and with those who were left behind in Jerusalem
   B. To illustrate the difference between believers and unbelievers
   C. To teach about incontinence
   D. To improve the diet of the residents of Judah

6. **How did God manifest his presence at the dedication of the temple?**
   A. In a pillar of cloud by day and a pillar of fire by night
   B. Fire came from heaven and consumed the sacrifice.
   C. A one-day supply of oil burned in the sacred lamp for eight days.
   D. By thunder and lightning

7. **How were the children of Israel guided in their forty years' wanderings in the wilderness?**
   A. By a pillar of cloud by day and a pillar of fire by night
   B. By blind camels

C. Through the visions of Moses and Aaron
D. By using Egyptian maps

8. How were the vast number of presents conveyed to King Solomon?
A. By the Queen of Sheba's camels
B. By the navies of Hiram and Tarshish
C. On the backs of elephants
D. Under a giant Christmas tree

9. **How was a miracle once performed to recover a borrowed axe?**
   A. By Moses when he parted the waters of the River Jordan
   B. By Elisha when he caused iron to swim
   C. By Elijah when he called down fire to destroy the sacred groves of Baal
   D. By Samuel when he used David's shadow to point to the missing axe

10. **How was the timber used in building Solomon's Temple conveyed to Jerusalem?**
   A. By sea on floats
   B. It was faxed
   C. On the backs of elephants
   D. In a caravan of donkey carts

FILL IN THE BLANKS

1. For I am not ashamed of the gospel of Christ, for it is ____________________ for everyone who believes, for the Jew first and also for the Greek.

2. Therefore, having ____________________, we have peace with God through our Lord Jesus Christ, through whom also we have access by faith

into this grace in which we stand, and rejoice in hope of the glory of God.

3. So then faith comes by hearing, and hearing by ______________________.

4. And if Christ is not ________, then our preaching is empty and your faith is also empty.

5. ____________, stand fast in the faith, be brave, be strong.

ANSWERS p. 298

6. For we ________ by faith, not by sight.

7. I have been __________ with Christ; it is no longer I who live, but Christ lives in me; and the life which I how live in the flesh I live by faith in the Son of God, who loved me and gave Himself for me.

8. For you are all sons of God through faith in Christ Jesus. For as many of you as ____________________ into Christ have put on Christ.

Q. How do we know Peter was a rich fisherman?

A. By his net income.

9. Therefore, as we have opportunity, let us do good to all, especially to those who are of the ________ ________________.

10. For by ________ you have been saved through faith, and that not of yourselves; it is the gift of God, not of works, lest anyone should boast.

WORD BANK

crucified	walk
household of faith	been justified by faith
Watch	the power of God to salvation
grace	risen
were baptized	the word of God

BIBLE MATH

When Jesus raised Lazarus from the dead, he taught an important lesson about eternal life. See what he told Martha, and us, by solving the puzzle below. Each answer is a number that matches a letter of the alphabet.

Put that letter in the blank next to the number and then in the quote at the bottom to find the missing words. The first one is done for you.

1st Word

Steps of Solomon's throne × 3	=	18	=	R
Psalms ÷ 30	=	___	=	___
Cows in Pharoah's dream + 5	=	___	=	___
Years Jacob worked for Rachel + 7	=	___	=	___
Years Aeneas was bedridden + 10	=	___	=	___
Commandments + 8	=	___	=	___
Gospels + 1	=	___	=	___
Branches on the vine in Pharoah's dream	=	___	=	___
Noah's days of rain ÷ 2	=	___	=	___
Abraham's angelic visitors × 3	=	___	=	___
Chapters in James × 3	=	___	=	___
Horsemen in Revelations + 10	=	___	=	___

2nd Word

Chapters in Ruth × 3	=	___	=	___
Sons of Adam & Eve × 3	=	___	=	___
Jars of water Jesus made into wine	=	___	=	___
Peter's denials + 2	=	___	=	___

3rd Word

Seals in Revelation – 5 = ___ = ___

Snakes in Eden + 4 = ___ = ___

Cities of Refuge × 2 = ___ = ___

Beatitudes – 1 = ___ = ___

Silver shekels paid for Joseph ÷ 4 = ___ = ___

Spies sent into Canaan + 10 = ___ = ___

Jesus' temptations + 2 = ___ = ___

Elders in Revelations – 5 = ___ = ___

4th Word

Tribes of Israel ÷ 3 = ___ = ___

Jonah's days inside the whale × 3 = ___ = ___

Spies hidden by Rahab + 3 = ___ = ___

I am the R ___ ___ ___ ___ ___ ___ ___ ___ ___ ___ ___ ___ ___ ___

and the ___ ___ ___ ___.

He who ___ ___ ___ ___ ___ ___ ___ ___ ___ ___ ___ in me will not

___ ___ ___.

Q. How do we know God has a sense of humor?

A. Because he can take a rib.

TRUE OR FALSE?

1. The Ark of the LORD was drawn by two milk cows when it was returned to Israel by the Philistines.

2. The Ephraimites, on one occasion, were known from the people of other tribes by their tribal dress.

3. The reason no sound was heard of hammering or chiseling in the building of Solomon's Temple was because all the workmen had gone deaf.

HOW ABOUT THAT!

There are more predictions in the Bible than there are commands. The number of predictions is 8,000, while the number of commands is 6,468.

4. The cedar used for building Solomon's Temple was transported on floats by sea to Joppa.

5. When the Jews asked for a king, God showed his displeasure by sending plague and famine.

6. Benhadad died by being hung by Haman.

7. Christ says we know the truth of his Word by asking the chief priests and rulers.

8. There are no differences in the LORD'S prayer in Luke and Matthew.

CROSSWORD PUZZLE

ANSWERS p. 303

Across

1. There is now no ____________ to those who are in Christ Jesus, who do not walk according to the flesh, but according to the Spirit (Romans 8:1).
5. If then you were raised with Christ, seek those things which are ____________, where Christ is, sitting at the right hand of God (Colossians 3:1).
8. Who is wise and ____________ among you? Let him show by good conduct that his works are done in the meekness of wisdom (James 3:13).
10. . . . to know the love of Christ which passes ____________; that you may be filled with all the fullness of God (Ephesians 3:19).
11. If any of you lacks ____________, let him ask of God, who gives to all liberally and without reproach, and it will be given to him (James 1:5).
12. In this is ____________, not that we ____________d God, but that He ____________d us and sent His Son to be the propitiation for our sins. Be______ed, if God so loved us, we also ought to ____________ one another. No one has seen God at any time. If we __________ one another, God abides in us, and His ______ has been perfected in us (1 John 4:10–12).
13. But God demonstrates His own love toward us, in that while we were still ____________, Christ died for us (Romans 5:8).

Down

1. Blessed be the God and Father of our Lord Jesus Christ, the Father of mercies and God of all ______,

who ____________s us in all our tribulation, that we may be able to ____________ those who are in trouble, with the ____________ with which we ourselves are ____________ed by God. For as the sufferings of Christ abound in us, so our consolation also abounds through Christ (2 Corinthians 1:3–5).

2. Be ____________ for nothing, but in everything by prayer and supplication, with thanksgiving, let your requests be made known to God (Philippians 4:6).
3. Let us therefore come boldly to the throne of ____________, that we may obtain mercy and find ____________ to help in time of need (Hebrews 4:16).
4. For God is not ____________ to forget your work and labor of love which you have shown toward His name, in that you have ministered to the saints, and do minister (Hebrews 6:10).
6. Now godliness with ____________ is great gain (1 Timothy 6:6).
7. Let each of you look out not only for his own ____________, but also for the ____________ of others (Philippians 2:4).
9. "As many as I love, I rebuke and chasten. Therefore be ____________ and repent" (Revelation 3:19).
10. Therefore, as the elect of God, holy and beloved, put on tender mercies, ____________, humility, meekness, longsuffering (Colossians 3:12).
11. And let us not grow ____________ while doing good, for in due season we shall reap if we do not lose heart (Galatians 6:9).

SHORT ANSWER

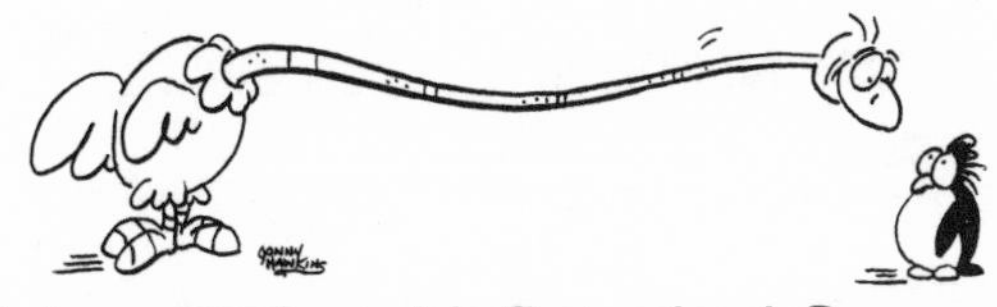

1. Where did Jesus perform his first miracle?

   ____

2. How many disciples did he have? ______________

3. What was his greatest sermon? ______________

4. Where did he often preach? ______________

5. Did he ever teach in the Temple? ______________

6. How many lepers did he once heal? ______________

7. How many came back to thank him? ______________

8. What friend did Jesus raise from the dead?

   ____

9. Where did Lazarus live? ______________

10. Name the sisters of Lazarus. ______________

WORD SCRAMBLE

How should we live as Christians? Jesus gave us the beatitudes as a guide for a spiritual life. Unscramble each of the words below to name those Jesus called blessed.

1. OROP NI TRIIPS ______ ___ __________
2. RONUM ______
3. EKEM _____
4. TISEOUGHR ___________
5. LICREFUM __________
6. THERPAERINU ____________
7. KAMAPEECRES ____________
8. DCUSERPETE ___________

BIBLE JEOPARDY

ANSWERS p. 305

$100 | $200 | $300 | $400 | DAILY DOUBLE | $500 | $600 | $700 | $800 | $900

Here are the answers. Do you know the questions?

1. This household feature is mentioned in Genesis 6:16.
2. Physicians are first named in this verse.
3. The plow is first mentioned in this phrase.
4. This man's letter was burned as it was read to King Jehoiakim.
5. This man said the first prayer on record.
6. These are the first words of Christ on record.

7. The first mention of a book is here.

8. Abraham purchased land from Ephron for this.

MATCHING

ANSWERS p. 305

Who asked these "How?" questions?

1. Lord God, how shall I know that I will inherit it?	a. Delilah
2. Quite obviously she is your wife; so how could you say, "She is my sister"?	b. Balaam
3. . . . how shall we clear ourselves?	c. Pharoah
4. How old are you?	d. King Rehoboam
5. How long will you refuse to humble yourself before Me? Let My people go, that they may serve Me.	e. The Philistines
6. How shall I curse whom God has not cursed? And how shall I denounce whom the Lord has not denounced?	f. Judah
7. Perhaps you dwell among us; so how can we make a covenant with you?	g. Abraham

8. How can you say, "I love you," when your heart is not with me?

h. Men of Israel

9. What shall we do with the ark of the Lord? Tell us how we should send it to its place.

i. Moses and Aaron

10. How do you advise me to answer these people?

j. Abimelech

WORD FIND

Find the names of Bible plants in the puzzle. Some are in a straight line up and down, some left to right, some on an angle (and backwards, of course). Circle each letter of each word. The letters left over spell out the puzzle's message.

S B D R U O G
E N R O O T R
E R E L P P A
D O N R A N P
T H I S T L E
C T V H E S S

Apple
Gourd
Grapes
Root
Seed
Thorn
Thistle
Vine

Jesus is the vine and we are the

__ __ __ __ __ __ __ __.

ENIGMA NO. 1

1. Who did his servants treacherously slay,
   As sleeping on his couch at noon he lay?

   ____

2. A prince who, with a missionary band,
   Went forth to preach throughout the Holy Land.

   ____

3. A town where mighty miracles were wrought,
   Which for its sin was to destruction brought?

   ____

4. Before what idol did a Syrian bend,
   Lest he his heathen master should offend?

   ____

5. Who, to withstand the Apostle's preaching sought,
   And on himself a fearful judgment brought

   ____

6. What did once save from death the human race,
   And for a year was their sole dwelling-place?

   ____

7. A prophet who was called in early youth,
And til old age he served the God of truth.

____

8. A mother who did early teach her boy
The way that leads to everlasting joy.

____

HOW ABOUT THAT!

About 30,000,000 copies of the complete text of the Bible, or of its principle sections, are distributed annually.

9. What king against the tribes of Israel fought,
Because a passage through his land they sought?

____

10. A word inscribed in Babel's regal hall;
Her impious king to penitence call.

____

11. What king would not take counsel of the wise,
But did his father's counselors despise?

____

12. What makes the gold with purest luster shine,
And is an emblem of God's Word Divine?

____

13. What beauteous creatures dwell in heaven above,
And visit earth on messages of love?

____

14. Who did, when Judah's tribe was borne away,
The ruler of the remnant basely slay?

____

15. Who brought good news, the apostle's heart to cheer,
When he was sore oppressed with grief and fear?

____

Q. How did Adam and Eve feel when expelled from the Garden of Eden?

A. They were really put out.

16. A blessed emblem of our Savior dear,

For those that trust in Him need never fear.

____

QUOTEFALL

Solve the puzzle by moving the letters to form words. The letters can only be moved to another place in the same column. Black boxes indicate the spaces between words. Each word begins in the left side of the box.

<table>
<tr><td></td><td></td><td></td><td>E</td><td></td><td></td><td>I</td><td></td><td>D</td><td></td><td>K</td><td></td><td>E</td><td></td><td>P</td><td></td><td></td></tr>
<tr><td>I</td><td>F</td><td></td><td>A</td><td>D</td><td>W</td><td>L</td><td>L</td><td>L</td><td></td><td>M</td><td>Y</td><td></td><td>H</td><td>I</td><td>M</td><td>M</td></tr>
<tr><td>E</td><td>R</td><td>H</td><td>R</td><td>N</td><td>L</td><td>A</td><td>N</td><td>E</td><td></td><td>V</td><td>E</td><td>E</td><td>E</td><td>A</td><td>T</td><td>Y</td></tr>
<tr><td>E</td><td>W</td><td>O</td><td>W</td><td>I</td><td>Y</td><td>O</td><td>N</td><td>L</td><td>O</td><td>O</td><td>V</td><td>F</td><td>S</td><td>M</td><td>H</td><td></td></tr>
<tr><td></td><td></td><td>■</td><td></td><td></td><td></td><td></td><td></td><td></td><td>■</td><td></td><td></td><td></td><td></td><td></td><td>■</td><td></td></tr>
<tr><td></td><td>■</td><td></td><td></td><td>■</td><td></td><td></td><td></td><td></td><td>■</td><td></td><td></td><td></td><td></td><td>■</td><td></td><td></td></tr>
<tr><td>■</td><td></td><td></td><td></td><td></td><td>■</td><td></td><td></td><td></td><td>■</td><td></td><td></td><td>■</td><td></td><td></td><td></td><td></td></tr>
<tr><td></td><td></td><td>■</td><td></td><td></td><td></td><td></td><td>■</td><td></td><td></td><td></td><td></td><td>■</td><td></td><td></td><td></td><td>■</td></tr>
</table>

CRAZY QUOTATIONS

The words in italics are scrambled versions of the words missing from the biblical passages that follow the story. Each phrase (e.g. *"As for Ken"*) is an anagram of a single word. Can you unscramble the words and fit them into the correct places?

ANSWERS p. 308

My Cousins, the Pilots

My father has three cousins—Ken, Jed, and James. All of them are pilots. James got his instructor's license first and then taught his brothers how to fly.

As for Ken, I knew him as amateur *and pro.* I was with him when he raced from Orange Grove *to Citrus Inn.*

I was watching the air races when Jed's plane caught fire. *I swear, "wee!"* before anyone else and I yelled, "*Eject, Jed.*" Fortunately, Jed obeyed "*James rule* number one: Always pack an extra parachute."

1. Jeremiah 5:7

"How shall I ____________ you for this?

Your children have ____________ Me

And sworn by those that are not gods.

2. Jeremiah 8:8

. . . they have ____________ the word of the Lord;

"How can you say, '____________,

And the law of the Lord is with us'?

3. Jeremiah 36:17

And they asked Baruch, saying, "Tell us now, how did you write all these words—at his [Jeremiah's] ____________?"

Q. How do we know that they did not play cards in the ark?

A. Because Noah sat on the deck.

4. Ezekiel 14:21

For thus says the Lord God: "How much more it shall be when I send My four severe judgments on ___________-the sword and famine and wild beasts and pestilence-to cut off man and beast from it?

SHORT ANSWER

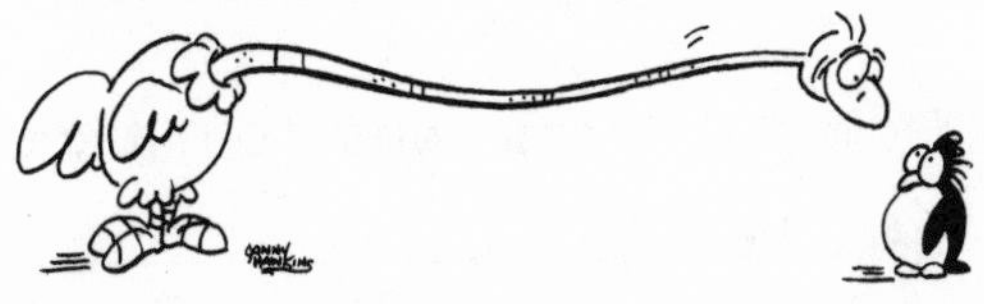

1. How many times is it recorded that our Lord was hungry? ___________

HOW ABOUT THAT!

The Bible was written by some 40 to 50 individuals, only one of whom (Luke) was a Gentile.

2. How many times was Paul shipwrecked? ___________

3. How many times does our Lord describe Himself as the "Last"? ___________

4. How do we know that Paul had a sister? ______________________________

5. How many sons had the prophet Isaiah? ______________

6. How does the New Testament say that a woman dishonors her head? ______________

7. How does a man who did not know how to read get a book? ______________

8. How many persons does the Bible describe as patriarchs? ______________

9. How do we know that the ancient Canaanites possessed engraved stones and molded images?

____

____

10. How do we know that no dwarf could officiate as a priest in Israel? ______________________________

____

ANSWERS TO: HOW?

MULTIPLE CHOICE

#	ANSWER	REFERENCE
1.	b.	2 Samuel 1:19–23
2.	a.	Leviticus 19:33–34
3.	c.	1 Samuel 17:50
4.	d.	2 Chronicles 22:1
5.	a.	Jeremiah 24:1, 3
6.	b.	2 Chronicles 7:1
7.	a.	Exodus 13:21
8.	b.	1 King 10:22
9.	b.	2 King 6:6
10.	a.	1 Kings 5:9

FILL IN THE BLANKS

#	ANSWER	REFERENCE
1.	the power of God to salvation	Romans 1:16–17
2.	been justified by faith	Romans 5:1–2
3.	the word of God	Romans 10:17
4.	risen	1 Corinthians 15:14
5.	Watch	1 Corinthians 16:13

#	ANSWER	REFERENCE
6.	walk	2 Corinthians 5:7
7.	crucified	Galatians 2:20
8.	were baptized	Galatians 3:26–27
9.	household of faith	Galatians 6:10
10.	grace	Ephesians 2:8–9

BIBLE MATH

#	ANSWER				
1.	Steps of Solomon's throne × 3	=	18	=	R
	Psalms ÷ 30	=	5	=	E
	Cows in Pharoah's dream + 5	=	19	=	S
	Years Jacob worked for Rachel + 7	=	21	=	U
	Years Aeneas was bedridden + 10	=	18	=	R
	Commandments + 8	=	18	=	R
	Gospels + 1	=	5	=	E
	Branches on the vine in Pharoah's dream	=	3	=	C
	Noah's days of rain ÷ 2	=	20	=	T
	Abraham's angelic visitors × 3	=	9	=	I
	Chapters in James × 3	=	15	=	O
	Horsemen in Revelations + 10	=	14	=	N

BIBLE MATH—cont'd

 # ANSWER

#			
2.	Chapters in Ruth × 3	= 12	= L
	Sons of Adam & Eve × 3	= 9	= I
	Jars of water Jesus made into wine	= 6	= F
	Peter's denials + 2	= 5	= E
3.	Seals in Revelation – 5	= 2	= B
	Snakes in Eden + 4	= 5	= E
	Cities of Refuge × 2	= 12	= L
	Beatitudes – 1	= 9	= I
	Silver shekels paid for Joseph ÷ 4	= 5	= E
	Spies sent into Canaan + 10	= 22	= V
	Jesus' temptations + 2	= 5	= E
	Elders in Revelations – 5	= 19	= S
4.	Tribes of Israel ÷ 3	= 4	= D
	Jonah's days inside the whale × 3	= 9	= I
	Spies hidden by Rahab + 3	= 5	= E

I am the R E S U R R E C T I O N

and the L I F E.

He who B E L I E V E S in me will not

D I E.

TRUE OR FALSE

#	ANSWER	REFERENCE
1.	True	1 Samuel 6:7
2.	False; By not being able to pronounce the "h" in the word "Shibboleth"	Judges 12:6
3.	False; Because every stone was chiseled, every beam sawed, every hole drilled, and every bolt fitted before being brought to the city	1 King 6:7
4.	True	2 Chronicles 2:16
5.	False; By sending thunder and rain	1 Samuel 12:17
6.	False; Smothered by Hazael	2 Kings 8:8
7.	False; He said, "If anyone wants to do His will, he shall know concerning the doctrine, whether it is from God or *whether* I speak on My own *authority.*"	John 7:17
8.	False; Matthew's version:	

Our Father in heaven,
Hallowed be Your name.
Your kingdom come.
Your will be done

TRUE OR FALSE—cont'd

# ANSWER	REFERENCE
On earth as *it is* in heaven. Give us this day our daily bread. And forgive us our debts, As we forgive our debtors. And do not lead us into temptation, But deliver us from the evil one.	Matthew 6:9–13
Luke's version: Our Father in heaven, Hallowed be Your name. Your kingdom come. Your will be done On earth as *it is* in heaven. Give us day by day our daily bread. And forgive us our sins, For we also forgive everyone who is indebted to us. And do not lead us into temptation, But deliver us from the evil one.	Luke 11:2–4

CROSSWORD PUZZLE

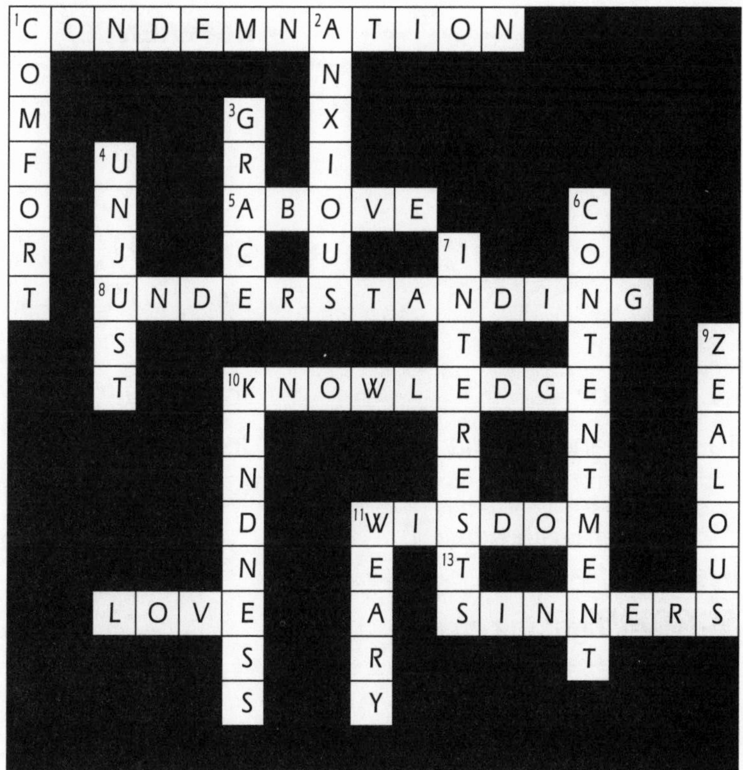

SHORT ANSWER

# ANSWER	REFERENCE
1. Wedding at Cana	John 2:1–11
2. 12	Matthew 10:1
3. Sermon on the Mount	Matthew 5—7

SHORT ANSWER—cont'd

#	ANSWER	REFERENCE
4.	By the seaside and roadside; out of doors	
5.	Yes	
6.	10	Luke 17:11–14
7.	1	Luke 17:15
8.	Lazarus	John 11:43–44
9.	Bethany	John 11:1
10.	Mary and Martha	John 11:1–2

WORD SCRAMBLE

#	ANSWER
1.	Poor in Spirit
2.	Mourn
3.	Meek
4.	Righteous
5.	Merciful
6.	Pure in heart
7.	Peacemakers
8.	Persecuted

BIBLE JEOPARDY

#	ANSWER	REFERENCE
1.	What are windows?	Genesis 6:16
2.	What is Genesis 50:2?	Genesis 50:2
3.	What is "You shall not plow with an ox and a donkey together."	Deuteronomy 22:10
4.	Who is Jeremiah?	Jeremiah 36: 21–23
5.	Who is Jacob?	Genesis 32:9–12
6.	What is, "Why did you seek Me? Did you not know I must be about my Father's business?	Luke 2:49
7.	Where is Exodus 17:14?	
8.	What is to have a place to bury Abraham's family members?	Genesis 23:16, 17

MATCHING

#	ANSWER	REFERENCE
1.	g.	Genesis 15:8
2.	j.	Genesis 26:9

MATCHING—cont'd

#	ANSWER	REFERENCE
3.	f.	Genesis 44:16
4.	c.	Genesis 47:8
5.	i.	Exodus 10:3
6.	b.	Numbers 23:8–9
7.	h.	Joshua 9:7
8.	a.	Judges 16:15
9.	e.	1 Samuel 6:2.
10.	d.	1 Kings 12:6

WORD FIND

After finding the names of Bible plants in the puzzle, the letters left over spell out the puzzle's message.

(S)	B	(D)	(R)	(U)	(O)	(G)
(E)	(N)	(R)	(O)	(O)	(T)	(R)
(E)	(R)	(E)	(L)	(P)	(P)	(A)
(D)	(O)	(N)	R	A	N	(P)
(T)	(H)	(I)	(S)	(T)	(L)	(E)
C	(T)	(V)	H	E	S	(S)

Apple
Gourd
Grapes
Root
Seed
Thorn
Thistle
Vine

Jesus is the vine and we are the

B R A N C H E S.

ENIGMA NO. 1

# ANSWER	REFERENCE
"INCREASE OUR FAITH." Luke 17:5	
1. **I**-sh-bosheth	2 Samuel 4
2. **N**-ethanel	2 Chronicles 17:7, 9
3. **C**-apernaum	Matthew 11:23
4. **R**-immon	2 Kings 5:18
5. **E**-lymas	Acts 13:8, 12.
6. **A**-rk	Genesis 7:11–13; 8:13–116
7. **S**-amuel	1 Samuel 3:12
8. **E**-unice	2 Timothy 1:5; 3:15.
9. **O**-g	Numbers 21:3
10. **U**-pharsin	Daniel 5:25
11. **R**-ehoboam	1 Kings 12:13
12. **F**-ire	Jeremiah 23:29
13. **A**-ngels	Hebrews 1:14
14. **I**-shmael	Jeremiah 41:2
15. **T**-itus	2 Corinthians 7:5–7
16. **H**-orn	Luke 1:69

Q. How long did Moses lie in the bulrushes?

A. Full length.

QUOTEFALL

			~~E~~			~~I~~		~~D~~		~~K~~		~~E~~		~~P~~		
~~I~~	~~F~~		~~A~~	~~D~~	~~W~~	~~L~~	~~L~~	~~L~~		~~M~~	~~Y~~		~~H~~	~~I~~	~~M~~	~~M~~
~~E~~	~~R~~	~~H~~	~~R~~	~~N~~	~~L~~	~~A~~	~~N~~	~~E~~		~~V~~	~~E~~	~~E~~	~~E~~	~~A~~	~~T~~	~~Y~~
~~E~~	~~W~~	~~O~~	~~W~~	~~I~~	~~Y~~	~~O~~	~~N~~	~~L~~	~~O~~	~~O~~	~~V~~	~~F~~	~~S~~	~~M~~	~~H~~	
I	F	■	A	N	Y	O	N	E	■	L	O	V	E	S	■	M
E	■	H	E	■	W	I	L	L	■	K	E	E	P	■	M	Y
■	W	O	R	D	■	A	N	D	■	M	Y	■	F	A	T	H
E	R	■	W	I	L	L	■	L	O	V	E	■	H	I	M	■

CRAZY QUOTATIONS

 # ANSWER **REFERENCE**

My Cousins, the Pilots

The unscrambled missing words are indicated by bold type.

1. "How shall I **pardon** you for this? Jeremiah 5:7
   Your children have **forsaken** Me
   And sworn by those that are not gods.
2. . . . they have **rejected** the word Jeremiah 8:8
   of the Lord;
   "How can you say, '**We are wise,**
   And the law of the Lord is with us'?

#	ANSWER	REFERENCE
3.	And they asked Baruch, saying, "Tell us now, how did you write all these words—at his [Jeremiah's] **instruction?**"	Jeremiah 36:17
4.	For thus says the Lord God: "How much more it shall be when I send My four severe judgments on **Jerusalem**—the sword and famine and wild beasts and pestilence—to cut off man and beast from it?	Ezekiel 14:21

SHORT ANSWER

#	ANSWER	REFERENCE
1.	Twice	Matthew 4:2; Matthew 21:18; Luke 4:2; Mark 11:12
2.	Three times	2 Corinthians 11:25 and Acts 27
3.	Three times	Revelation 1:17; 2:8; 22:13
4.	Because she had a son	Acts 23:16
5.	Two	Isaiah 7:3 and 8:3

SHORT ANSWER—cont'd

#	ANSWER	REFERENCE
6.	By praying bare-headed	1 Corinthians 11:5
7.	It was delivered to him.	Isaiah 29:12
8.	Fourteen (David, Abraham, and Jacob's 12 sons)	Acts 2:29 and 7:8–9; Hebrews 7:4
9.	Because they were destroyed in the conquest of Canaan	Numbers 33:52
10.	It is stated in the regulations and conduct of priests.	Leviticus 21:20

Getting the Quotes: Old Testament

MULTIPLE CHOICE

1. **Finish the sentence: "A little that a righteous man has ____________."**
   A. becomes a treasure in his hands
   B. makes that man a little righteous
   C. is better than the riches of many wicked
   D. is all spent on hats

2. **What is the rest of the proverb, "Pride goes before destruction, ____________"?**
   A. and a haughty spirit before a fall
   B. and ignorance before bliss
   C. and folly before a foolish word
   D. and joy before a repentant heart

ANSWERS p. 338

3. **Finish the sentence from the Psalms: "O send out Your light and Your truth. ____________."**
   A. Bless me in this way
   B. Be not far from me
   C. But please not the really bright light, for it burns
   D. Let them lead me

4. **What is the rest of the proverb, "There is a way that seems right to a man, but ____________."**
   A. he should stop and ask for directions
   B. its end is the way of death
   C. it will surely lead him astray
   D. it is not the way of the LORD

5. **What is the rest of the saying in Ecclesiastes: "A living dog is better than ________."**
   A. three shekels of barley
   B. a rabid squirrel
   C. a diseased mule
   D. a dead lion

6. **Complete this sentence from Habakkuk: "The LORD is in His holy temple. ________."**
   A. Bow down and worship
   B. Let all the earth keep silence before him
   C. Do not disturb
   D. Let us gather together and praise him

7. **Finish the proverb: "A friend loves at all times, and ________."**
   A. a brother is born for adversity
   B. a lover is always a friend
   C. an enemy hates always
   D. you don't have any

8. **Finish the quotation: "God is our refuge and strength, ________."**
   A. and he is a mighty fortress
   B. a never-ending ice cream sandwich

Q. What simple affliction brought about the death of Samson?

A. Falling Arches

C. a very present help in trouble
D. quick to forgive and slow to become angry

9. Finish the quotation: "This God is our God for ever and ever. He will be ____________."
A. here forever and ever
B. our guide even to death
C. our God and we will be his people
D. bigger than life

10. Finish the quotation: "Create in me a clean heart, O God; and ________________________."
A. restore unto me the joy of my salvation
B. wash away all my sin
C. create in my house a clean room
D. renew a right spirit within me

FILL IN THE BLANKS

Supply the missing part of each quotation from Scripture.

1. "When my father and my mother forsake me, __________________."

2. "The LORD is good, a stronghold in the day of trouble, and He ________________________

3. "The harvest is past, the summer is ended, and ____________________________."

4. "Multitudes, multitudes ____________________."

5. "This is the day the LORD has made, ____________
____________."

6. "Trust in the LORD with all Your heart ____________
____________."

7. "Weeping may endure for a night, but ____________
____________."

8. "When you make a vow to God ____________
____________"

9. "Dishonest scales are an abomination to the LORD ____________."

10. "Hope deferred ____________________."

BIBLE MATH

ANSWERS p. 339

When God changed people's lives, He sometimes changed their names too! Solve the puzzle below and find out who our Old Testament hero was before and after! Each answer is a number that matches a letter of the alphabet (A=1, B=2, C=3 . . .). Put that letter in the blank next to the number and then in the quote at the bottom to find the missing words. The first one is done for you.

1st Word

Plagues on Egypt	= 10	= J
Gospels – 3	= ___	= ___
New Testament books ÷ 9	= ___	= ___
Seals in Revelation + 8	= ___	= ___
Snakes in Eden × 2	= ___	= ___

2nd Word

Springs at Elim – 3	= ___	= ___
Chapters in Judges – 2	= ___	= ___
Jars of water Jesus made into wine × 3	= ___	= ___
Peter's denials – 2	= ___	= ___
Horns of the Beast ÷ 2	= ___	= ___
Jesse's sons + 4	= ___	= ___

3rd Word

Verses in Jude – 6	= ___	= ___
Commandments × 2	= ___	= ___
Steps of Solomon's throne – 3	= ___	= ___
Job's friends × 7	= ___	= ___
Deacons chosen in Acts 6	= ___	= ___
Chapters in Ruth + 3	= ___	= ___
Old Testament books – 18	= ___	= ___
Letters to Timothy + 3	= ___	= ___
Horsemen in Revelation	= ___	= ___

4th Word

Patriarchs + 3 = ___ = ___

Judas' silver pieces – 8 = ___ = ___

Sons of Noah + 2 = ___ = ___

Cities of Refuge × 3 = ___ = ___

Jesus' days in the tomb = ___ = ___

Loaves that fed 5,000 × 3 = ___ = ___

Beatitudes + 3 = ___ = ___

Disciples – 7 = ___ = ___

Your name will no longer be J___ ___ ___ ___ ___ but

___ ___ ___ ___ ___ ___ because you have

___ ___ ___ ___ ___ ___ ___ ___ ___ ___ with God and

___ ___ ___ ___ ___ ___ ___ ___.

TRUE OR FALSE?

1. Amos, the prophet, was a herdsman of Tekoa.

2. The father of Mahershalal-hash-baz was Jeremiah.

3. Gad, the high priest, made and worshipped idols.

4. King Ahaz led a victorious army that took as trophies of war two hundred thousand captives and much spoil.

5. Obed, the prophet, advised that a captive host return to their own country by their victors.

6. King Solomon took pride in the census of his people.

7. Elijah, together with the Shunamite widow and her two sons, engaged in a legitimate, remarkable, and profitable oil speculation.

HOW ABOUT THAT!

The first printed Bible divided into verses was a Latin edition by Pagninus, printed in 1528.

8. King Saul traded in apes and peacocks.

9. Ezekiel, bereft of his best earthly friend, did not grow weak in compliance with the command of God.

10. The prophets Elisha and Nathan reproved King David.

CROSSWORD PUZZLE

Across

2. ____________ to Me, and I will ____________ to you. (Malachi 3:7)

5. The Sun of Righteousness shall arise with healing in His ____________. (Malachi 4:2)

6. Blessed is he who considers the ____________. (Psalms 41:1)

7. Thanksgiving and the voice of ______________. (Isaiah 51:3)
8. But the mercy of the LORD is from everlasting to everlasting on those who______________ Him. (Psalm 103:17)
9. For He will abundantly ______________. (Isaiah 55:7)
10. Shall abide under the ______________ of the Almighty. (Psalm 91:1)
11. Those who sow in ______________. (Psalm 126:5)
12. God is our ______________ and strength. (Psalm 46:1, 2)
13. And He shall give you the ______________ of your heart. (Psalm 37:4)

Down

1. How pleasant it is for brethren to dwell together in ______________. (Psalm 133:1)
2. You love ______________ and hate wickedness. (Psalm 45:7)
3. The LORD is ______________ to all who call upon Him. (Psalm 145:18)
4. You shall be called by a new ______________. (Isaiah 62:12)
7. What can ______________ do to me? (Psalm 56:11)
8. These things I will do for them, and not ______________ them. (Isaiah 42:16)

SHORT ANSWER

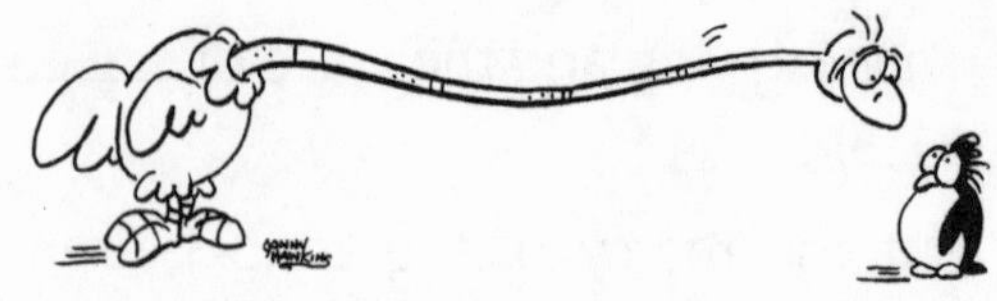

Give the Scripture reference for the following verses.

1. Where is the declaration, "Man looks at the outward appearance, but the LORD looks at the heart"?

   ____

2. Where is the wise reminder, "The fear of man brings a snare"? ______________________________

3. What is the source of the familiar metaphor, "an arm of flesh"? ______________________________

4. Where is the solemn warning, "be sure your sin will find you out"? ______________________________

5. Where is the humane injunction, "A righteous man regards the life of his animal"? ________________

6. Where is the LORD described as, "glorious in holiness, fearful in praise, doing wonders"? __________

____

HOW ABOUT THAT!

The first complete English version of the Bible divided into verses was the Geneva Bible, printed in 1560.

7. Where is it said, "Those who honor me I will honor, and those who despise me shall be lightly esteemed"?

____

8. Where does the command to "love and serve the Lord with all the heart and with all the soul" first appear? ________________________

9. Where is the command to "love the stranger"?

____

10. Where does it say, "love your neighbor as yourself"?

____

WORD BANK

Deuteronomy 10:12;11:1

Proverbs 29:25 Jeremiah 17:5

1 Samuel 16:7 2 Chronicles

Deuteronomy 10:19 Exodus 15:11

Proverbs 12:10 1 Samuel 2:30

Leviticus 19:18, 34

WORD SCRAMBLE

How did God call to His people in the Old Testament? Unscramble each of the words below to name a few of God's chosen prophets.

1. COHEN _ _ _ _ _
2. ORANA _ _ _ _ _ _
3. TAHNAN _ _ _ _ _
4. KOAZD _ _ _ _ _

5. HAAJIH _ _ _ _ _ _

6. UJHE _ _ _ _

7. AJELIH _ _ _ _ _ _

8. EJOL _ _ _ _

9. ASHIAI _ _ _ _ _ _

10. IGAHGA _ _ _ _ _ _

11. HADOAIB _ _ _ _ _ _ _

12. CHAMI _ _ _ _ _

ANSWERS p. 343

BIBLE JEOPARDY

$100	$200	$300	$400	DAILY DOUBLE	$500	$600	$700	$800	$900

Here the answers. Do you know the questions?

1. He was the first king of Israel.
2. He planted the first vineyard.
3. He was the first disciple Jesus chose.
4. He was the first archer mentioned in the Bible.
5. He said, "Man does not live by bread only . . .
6. He was the first judge of Israel.
7. He was the first polygamist.

8. She was the first daughter mentioned by name.

9. She was the first person to use a pseudenym.

MATCHING

1. "Can the Ethiopian change his skin

2. "The LORD is near to those who have a broken heart,

a. the LORD delivers him out of them all."

b. living La Vida Loca."

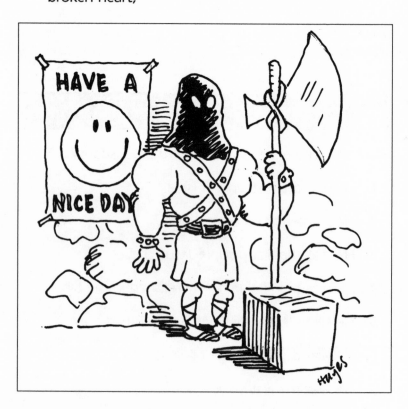

3. "There the wicked cease from troubling, and

4. "Do not say,

5. "Many are the afflictions of the righteous, but

6. "The eyes of the LORD are in every place

7. "Upside, inside out

8. "The soul who sins

9. "Better is a dinner of vegetables where love is

10. "Man is born to trouble

c. why were the former days better than these? For you do not inquire wisely concerning this."

d. 'There the weary are at rest.' "

e. as the sparks fly upward."

f. or the leopard its spots?"

g. and saves such as have a contrite spirit."

h. keeping watch on the evil and the good."

i. than a fatted calf with hatred."

j. shall die."

Q. What animal could Noah not trust?

A. The Cheetah

WORD FIND

Find the names of men and women of the Old Testament listed below in the puzzle.

S A E H A R R O M O G D B
I L B F D E K C I W E R O
M I E R I L O T D L I B S
T S J G A N W Z L M E A E
N H X E N M K A S Y R S D
A M E B C A C T E A I A R
N A R C S I O D H Y A L A
E E I F C N F C R K R T L
V L F A E F S I A A U U L
O I A T A H Z A R N G G I
C S D I R A M Q R C A A P
I M T J M O D O S A A A H
U H B M A H A R B A I S N

Abraham
Abram
Angels
Brimstone
Called
Canaan
Covenant
Faith
Fire
Gomorrah
Hagar
Isaac
Ishmael
Knife
Lot
Obeyed
Pillar
Ram
Sacrifice
Salt
Sarah
Sarai
Sodom
Ur
Wicked

ENIGMA NO. 1

The initials will give a promise of consolation.

The city in the siege of which Uriah the Hittite was killed.
The place where Baal-zebub was worshipped.
The metropolis of Ahab.
The city built by Solomon in the wilderness.
The Father of twelve princes.
The invader from whom Saul delivered Jabesh Gilead.
The place to which Jonah thought to flee.
The rebuilder of Jericho.
The man who rescued Jeremiah from the dungeon.
The author of the last chapter of Proverbs.
The mountain ascended by David when he fled from Absalom.
The mother of Armoni and Mephibosheth.
The birth place of Abraham's steward.

MATCHING

1. "Ho, every one who thirsts	a. Israel does not know, my people do not consider."
2. "A wise son makes	b. the glory of God."
3. "O Come, let us worship and bow down,	c. in pleasant places."

4. "The Lord knows the way of the righteous, but

5. "The fool has said in his heart,

6. "The fear of the Lord

7. "The ox knows his owner, and the donkey his master's crib: but

d. learn to do well."

e. come to the waters."

f. is the beginning of wisdom."

g. 'There is no God.'"

HOW ABOUT THAT!

More than 500 million portions of Scripture are distributed annually.

8. "The lines are fallen to me

9. "Cease to do evil,

10. "The heavens declare ______ and the firmament shows ______

h. let us kneel before the LORD our Maker."

i. the way of the ungodly shall perish."

i. a father glad."

k. his handiwork."

WORD GAME

Change just one letter in each move to make a new word. See if you can make the word "lion" become the word "lamb."

ANSWERS p. 347

Ex.: C A N

C A T

C O T

H O T

L I O N

__ __* __ __

__ __ __ __*

__ __ __* __

__ __* __ __

__ __ __ __*

__ __ __* __

L A M B

Q. What do we have that Adam never had?

A. Parents.

SHORT ANSWER

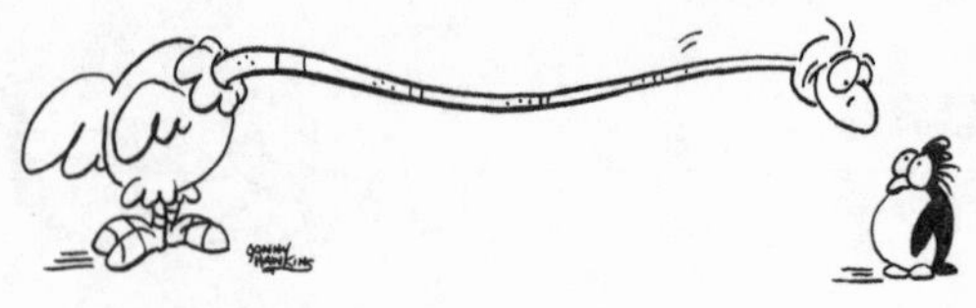

1. What does the proverb say of one "who spares his rod"? ______________________

2. Finish the proverb: "The path of the just is like the shining light," ______________________

3. What is the refrain of Psalm 136, ending each of its twenty-six verses? ______________________

4. Finish the proverb: "Keep your heart with all diligence; for ______________________."

5. Complete the proverb: "There is a way that seems right to a man but ____________________."

6. Finish the sentence: "Many sorrows shall be to the wicked; but ____________________."

HOW ABOUT THAT!

The Caxton Memorial Bible was printed and bound in twelve hours in 1877. Only one hundred copies were made.

7. Complete the command in Leviticus, "You shall keep my sabbaths ____________________."

8. How does the Psalm begin which describes the impossibility of running away from God? ____________________

____

9. Finish the proverb: "Righteousness exalts a nation, but ____________________."

10. Finish the sentence in Ecclesiastes: "When goods increase, ____________________."

FILL IN THE BLANKS

Supply the missing part of the quotations from Scripture.

1. "The LORD is good, a stronghold in the day of trouble, ______________________________."

2. "______________________ and when he is old, he will not depart from it."

3. "The LORD is my ______________; Whom shall I fear? The LORD is ______________; Of whom shall I be afraid?"

4. "But those who wait on the LORD Shall renew their strength; ______________, They shall run and not be weary, They shall walk and not faint."

5. "Trust in the LORD with all your heart, And lean not on your own understanding; In all your ways acknowledge Him, ______________."

6. "Surely in vain the net is spread______________"

7. "The generous soul ______________"?

8. "______________ in the beauty of holiness"?

9. Complete the following: "if My people who are called by My name will humble themselves, and pray and seek My face, and turn from their wicked ways, ______________."

10. "You shall love the LORD your God with all ______________

______________."

11. "You shall ________ your neighbor ______________.

MULTIPLE CHOICE

1. **What is the source of the Ten Commandments?**
   - **A.** God gave them to Noah.
   - **B.** God gave them to Moses.
   - **C.** Jesus gave them to us.
   - **D.** They were first found in the Ark of the Covenant.
   - **E.** Dr. Laura

2. **What happened to the prophet Jonah?**
   - **A.** He was thrown into a den of lions.
   - **B.** He was thrown into a fiery furnace.
   - **C.** He was tarred and feathered and sent to the county line.
   - **D.** He was swallowed by a giant fish.
   - **E.** He was taken to heaven in a fiery chariot.

3. **What happened to the prophet Daniel?**
   - **A.** He was thrown into a den of lions.
   - **B.** He was thrown into a fiery furnace.
   - **C.** He was given dancing lessons by Shadrach, Meshach, and Abed-nego.

Q. What animal in the ark had the smallest appetite?

A. The moth. He just eats holes

D. He was swallowed by a giant fish.
E. He was elected to the Council of Elders.

4. What ruse did Moses' mother use to save him from being killed by the evil pharaoh?
A. She hid him in a manger in the stable.
B. She hid him in a basket floating in the river.
C. She sent him out of Egypt with a caravan of traders.
D. She sent him to the Land of Nod.
E. She turned him into a newt.

ANSWERS p. 349

5. What happened to the three men Shadrach, Meshach and Abednego?
A. They were thrown into a den of lions.
B. They were thrown into a fiery furnace.
C. They were swallowed by a giant fish.
D. They were hidden in a basket floating in the river.
E. They changed their names to Moe, Larry, and Curly.

Cliff Leitch (<http://www.twopaths.com/>http://twopaths.com) as adapted by LDS.

ANSWERS TO: GETTING THE QUOTES: OLD TESTAMENT

MULTIPLE CHOICE

#	ANSWER	REFERENCE
1.	c.	Psalm 37:16
2.	a.	Proverbs 16:18
3.	d.	Psalm 43:3
4.	b.	Proverbs 14:12
5.	d.	Ecclesiastes 9:4
6.	b.	Habakkuk 2:20
7.	a.	Proverbs 17:17
8.	c.	Psalm 46:1–2
9.	b.	Psalm 48:14
10.	d.	Psalm 51:10

FILL IN THE BLANKS

#	ANSWER	REFERENCE
1.	"then the LORD will take care of me."	Psalm 27:10
2.	"knows those who trust in Him."	Nahum 1:7

#	ANSWER	REFERENCE
3.	"we are not saved."	Jeremiah 8:20
4.	"in the valley of decision."	Joel 3:14
5.	"We will rejoice and be glad in it."	Psalm 118:24
6.	"and lean not on Your own understanding."	Proverbs 3:5
7.	"joy comes in the morning."	Psalms 30:5
8.	"do not delay to pay it;"	Ecclesiastes 5:4
9.	"But a just weight is His delight."	Proverbs 11:1
10.	"makes the heart sick."	Proverbs 13:12

BIBLE MATH

#	ANSWER				
1.	Plagues on Egypt	=	10	=	J
	Gospels – 3	=	1	=	A
	New Testament books ÷ 9	=	3	=	C
	Seals in Revelation + 8	=	15	=	O
	Snakes in Eden × 2	=	2	=	B
2.	Springs at Elim – 3	=	9	=	I
	Chapters in Judges – 2	=	19	=	S
	Jars of water Jesus made into wine × 3	=	18	=	R

BIBLE MATH—cont'd

 # ANSWER

#	Clue		Number		Letter
	Peter's denials – 2	=	1	=	A
	Horns of the Beast ÷ 2	=	5	=	E
	Jesse's sons + 4	=	12	=	L
3.	Verses in Jude – 6	=	19	=	S
	Commandments × 2	=	20	=	T
	Steps of Solomon's throne – 3	=	18	=	R
	Job's friends × 7	=	21	=	U
	Deacons chosen in Acts 6	=	7	=	G
	Chapters in Ruth + 3	=	7	=	G
	Old Testament books – 18	=	12	=	L
	Letters to Timothy + 3	=	5	=	E
	Horsemen in Revelation	=	4	=	D
4.	Patriarchs + 3	=	15	=	O
	Judas' silver pieces – 8	=	22	=	V
	Sons of Noah + 2	=	5	=	E
	Cities of Refuge × 3	=	18	=	R
	Jesus' days in the tomb	=	3	=	C
	Loaves that fed 5,000 × 3	=	15	=	O
	Beatitudes + 3	=	13	=	M
	Disciples – 7	=	5	=	E

ANSWER

Your name will no longer be J A C O B but I S R A E L because you have S T R U G G L E D with God and O V E R C O M E.

TRUE OR FALSE

# ANSWER	REFERENCE
1. True	Amos 1:1; 7:14
2. False; Isaiah	Isaiah 8:1, 4
3. False; Aaron	Exodus 32:4; 20
4. True	2 Chronicles 28:8
5. True	2 Chronicles 28:9
6. False; David	2 Samuel 24:1
7. False; Elisha	2 Kings 4:1–7
8. False; Solomon	1 Kings 10:22
9. True	Ezekiel 24:16
10. False; Gad and Nathan	2 Samuel 24:11–19; 2 Samuel 12; 1 Chronicles 21

CROSSWORD PUZZLE

					1 U		2 R	E	T	U	R	3 N
	4 N				N		I					E
	A			5 W	I	N	G	S				A
	M				T		H		6 P	O	O	R
7 M	E	L	O	D	Y		T					
A							E					
N		8 F	E	A	R		O					
		O					U					
9 P	A	R	D	O	N		10 S	H	A	D	O	W
		S					N					
11 T	E	A	R	S		12 R	E	F	U	G	E	
		K					S					
	13 D	E	S	I	R	E	S					

SHORT ANSWER

 # ANSWER

1. 1 Samuel 16:7
2. Proverbs 29:25
3. 2 Chronicles 32:8

#	ANSWER
4.	Jeremiah 17:5
5.	Proverbs 12:10
6.	Exodus 15:11
7.	1 Samuel 2:30
8.	Deuteronomy 10:12; 11:1
9.	Deuteronomy 10:19
10.	Leviticus 19:18, 34

WORD SCRAMBLE

#	ANSWER
1.	Enoch
2.	Aaron
3.	Nathan
4.	Zadok
5.	Ahijah
6.	Jehu
7.	Elijah
8.	Joel
9.	Isaiah
10.	Haggai
11.	Obadiah
12.	Micah

BIBLE JEOPARDY

#	ANSWER
1.	Who is Saul?
2.	Who is Noah?
3.	Who is Simon Peter?
4.	Who is Ishmael?
5.	Who is Moses?
6.	Who is Othniel?
7.	Who is Lamech?
8.	Who is Naamah?
9.	Who is Esther?

MATCHING

#	ANSWER	
1.	f.	Jeremiah 13:23
2.	g.	Psalm 34:18
3.	d.	Job 3:17
4.	c.	Ecclesiastes 7:10
5.	a.	Psalm 34:19
6.	h.	Proverbs 15:13
7.	b.	

#	ANSWER
8. j.	Ezekiel 18:4
9. i.	Proverbs 15:17
10. e.	Job 5:7

WORD FIND

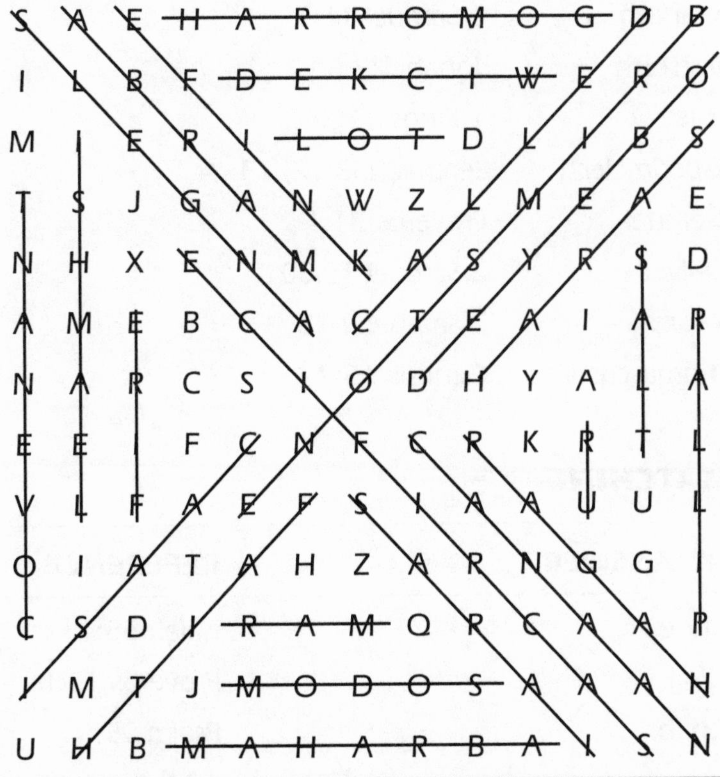

ENIGMA NO. 1

ANSWER	REFERENCE
"REST IN THE LORD" Psalm 37:7.	
R-abbath	2 Samuel 11:1
E-knon	2 Kings 1:2
S-amaria	1 Kings 16:29
T-admor	1 Kings 9:18
I-shmael	Genesis 17:20
N-ahash	1 Samuel 11:1
T-arshish	Jonah 1:3
H-iel	1 Kings 16:34
E-bedmelech	Jeremiah38:12, 13
L-emuel	Proverbs 31:1
O-livet	2 Samuel 15:30
R-ipzah	2 Samuel 21:8
D-amascus	Genesis 15:2

MATCHING

# ANSWER	REFERENCE
1. e.	Isaiah 55:1
2. j.	Proverbs 10:1
3. h.	Psalm 95:6

# ANSWER	REFERENCE
4. i.	Psalm 1:6
5. g.	Psalm 14:1
6. f.	Psalm 111:10
7. a.	Isaiah 1:3
8. c.	Psalm 16:6
9. d.	Isaiah 1:16–17
10. b., k.	Psalm 19:1

WORD GAME

ANSWER
L I O N
L O O N
L O O K
L O C K
L A C K
L A C E
L A M E
L A M B

SHORT ANSWER

#	ANSWER	REFERENCE
1.	He "hates his son."	Proverbs 13:24
2.	"That shines ever brighter unto the perfect day."	Proverbs 4:18
3.	"For his mercy endures for ever."	
4.	"Out of it spring the issues of life."	Proverbs 4:23
5.	"Its end is the way of death."	Proverbs 14:12
6.	"he who trusts in the LORD, mercy shall surround him."	Psalms 32:10
7.	"and reverence my sanctuary."	Leviticus 19:30
8.	"O LORD, You have searched me and known me."	Psalm 139:1
9.	"sin is a reproach to any people."	Proverbs 14:34
10.	"They increase who eat them."	Ecclesiastes 5:11

FILL IN THE BLANKS

#	ANSWER	REFERENCE
1.	"And He knows those who trust in Him."	Nahum 1:7

#	ANSWER	REFERENCE
2.	"Train up a child in the way he should go"	Proverbs 22:6
3.	"light and my salvation;" "the strength of my life;"	Psalm 27:1
4.	"They shall mount up with wings like eagles"	Isaiah 40:31
5.	"And He shall direct Your paths."	Proverbs 3:5–6
6.	"In the sight of any bird."	Proverbs 1:17
7.	"shall be made rich."	Proverbs 11:25
8.	"Worship the LORD."	Psalms 29:2
9.	"then I will hear from heaven, and will forgive their sin and heal their land."	2 Chronicles 7:14
10.	"your heart, with all your soul, and with all your strength."	Deuteronomy 6:5
11.	"love," "as yourself."	Leviticus 19:18

MULTIPLE CHOICE

#	ANSWER
1.	b.
2.	d.
3.	a.
4.	b.
5.	b.

Getting the Quotes: New Testament

MULTIPLE CHOICE

1. **After what miracle did the astonished multitude say of Christ, "He has done all things well"?**
   A. the raising of Lazarus
   B. changing water into wine
   C. the healing of the deaf man with an impediment in his speech
   D. casting out the evil spirits from a demon-possessed man

2. **With what saying did Christ lament the shortage of evangelists?**
   A. "You are the salt of the earth."
   B. "A city set on a hill cannot be hidden."
   C. "Go into all the world and preach the gospel."
   D. "The harvest truly is plentiful, but the laborers are few."

3. **In what city were the converts urged, "that with purpose of heart they would continue with the Lord"?**
   A. Jerusalem
   B. Nazareth
   C. Philippi
   D. Antioch of Syria

ANSWERS
p. 381

4. **What did Paul urge us to present to God as a living sacrifice?**
   A. our bodies
   B. our money

C. our children
D. our shoes

5. **What did Paul say is required in stewards?**
   A. that they be financially secure
   B. that they be trained in banking and investments
   C. that they are faithful
   D. that they make a mean stew

HOW ABOUT THAT!

The Thumb Bible, 1670, was one inch square and half an inch thick. It could be read only with a magnifying glass.

6. **What did Christ say would happen to any man who was ashamed of him?**
   A. He would be cast into the lake of fire.
   B. He would live to regret it.
   C. He had many other things of which to be ashamed.
   D. Jesus would be ashamed of him when he returned.

7. **Just before what did Christ say that he was the light of the world?**

A. just before sunrise on Palm Sunday
B. just before opening the eyes of a man born blind
C. just before sending his disciples to preach the Gospel
D. just before he left the disciples on the road to Emmaus

8. In what connection did Paul write, "A little leaven leavens the whole lump"?
A. when dictating some of his favorite recipes
B. when explaining the power of the Gospel
C. when protesting an evil person in one of the churches
D. when instructing Christians not to marry non-Christians

9. What led Christ to say that he who was not against them was on their side"?
A. when his disciples disparaged the followers of John the Baptist
B. when he was invited to preach at the synagogue in Nazareth
C. when his disciples interfered with a stranger who was casting out demons
D. when he instructed his disciples how to play "Red Rover"

10. When Jesus cast out an evil spirit who had resisted his disciples, he explained that:
A. "This kind can come out by nothing but prayer and fasting."
B. "Nothing is impossible to him who believes."

C. "Do not blaspheme against the Holy Spirit."

D. "You have not because you ask not."

FILL IN THE BLANKS

1. Finish the quotation: "If anyone desires to come after Me, let him deny himself ________."

2. Complete Paul's sentence: "We then who are strong ought to bear with the scruples of the weak, and ________."

3. Finish the quotation from Romans: "Whoever calls on the name of the Lord ________."

4. Finish Paul's great sentence: "All things are yours; whether Paul, or ________ ________."

5. Finish James's sentence: "Draw near to God, and ________."

6. Complete Paul's sentence: ". . . the letter kills, but ________."

7. Finish the phrase from Hebrews: "Jesus Christ is the same ________."

8. Fill in the blanks: "Whoever desires to save ______, ______________ but whoever loses ________________ shall save it."

9. "______________, who do not walk according to the flesh, but according to the Spirit."

10. "Who shall ______________? Shall tribulation, or distress, or persecution, or famine, or nakedness, or peril, or sword?"

11. "For to me, to live ______________________."

12. "Let no one despise your youth, but be an example to the believers in ____________."

HOW ABOUT THAT!

By the age of ten, Abraham Lincoln had read the entire Bible three times!

13. "Let each of you look out not only for his own interests, ______________________."

14. "Therefore, my beloved, as you have always obeyed, not as in my presence only, but now much more in my absence, ____________________."

15. "Do not love the world or the things in the world. If anyone loves the world, __________________."

BIBLE MATH

What did Jesus teach about his kingdom? Find out by solving the puzzle below. Each answer is a number that matches a letter of the alphabet (A=1, B=2, C=3 . . .). Put that letter in the blank next to the number and then in the quote at the bottom to find the missing words. The first one is done for you.

1st Word

Commandments + 1 = 11 = K

Stones picked up by David + 4 = ___ = ___

Deacons chosen in Acts 6 × 2 = ___ = ___

Kings of the Amorites + 2 = ___ = ___

Lazarus' sisters × 2 = ___ = ___

Job's friends × 5 = ___ = ___

Abraham's angelic visitors + 10 = ___ = ___

2nd Word

Spies sent into Canaan – 5 = ___ = ___

Old Testament books ÷ 2 = ___ = ___

Abijah's wives – 10 = ___ = ___

3rd Word

Jesus' days in the desert – 17 = ___ = ___

New Testament books ÷ 3 = ___ = ___

Silver shekels paid for Joseph = ___ = ___

Leaders of men in Micah 5 = ___ = ___

Jonah's days inside the whale × 3 = ___ = ___

Jesse's sons + 6 = ___ = ___

4th Word

Elders in Revelation + 1 = ___ = ___

Lepers healed by Jesus + 5 = ___ = ___

Chapters in Judges = ___ = ___

The K___ ___ ___ ___ ___ ___ ___ of ___ ___ ___

is ___ ___ ___ ___ ___ ___ ___ ___ ___.

TRUE OR FALSE

1. The apostle John wrote, "Faith without works is dead."

2. Good and evil are the two masters that Christ said no man can serve at the same time.

3. James was speaking of the power of the tongue when he wrote, "See how great a forest a little fire kindles!"

4. Christ's point of the parable of the speck and the plank is that you should take care of your own family before you try to help another's.

5. In Paul's most hopeful saying he taught, "All things work together for good to those who love God."

6. Paul believed that there is no other foundation for the Christian faith than the Bible.

7. Lack of persistence is the reason that James gave for failures to obtain answers to prayer.

8. To the church of Ephesus Jesus says in Revelation, "You have a little strength, and have kept my word, and have not denied my name."

9. To the dead son of the widow in Nain Christ said, "Young man, I say to you, Arise"?

10. It was in Jerusalem that Christ said, "A prophet is not without honor except in his own country."

CROSSWORD PUZZLE

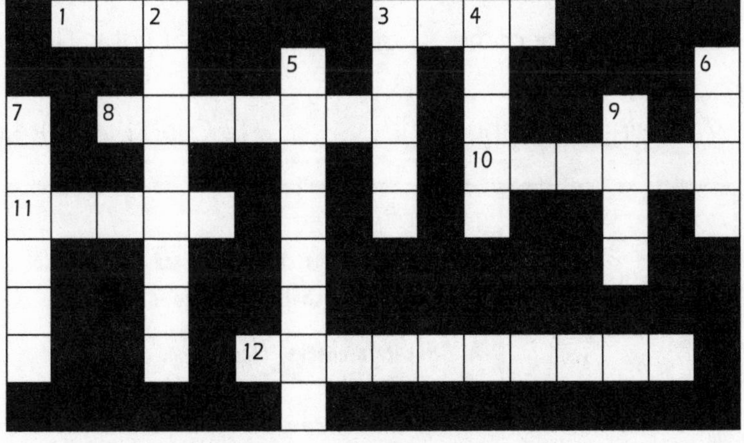

Across:

1. ______________ is light and in Him is no darkness. (1 John 1:05)
3. ____________ while you have the light. (John 12:35)
8. He who loves his ____________ abides in the light. (1 John 2:10)
10. Saw on the way a light from ____________. (Acts 26:13)
11. Let your light _______ before men. (Matthew 5:16)
12. What ____________ can light have with darkness. (2 Corinthians 6:14)

Down:

2. A light to those who are in ____________. (Romans 2:19)
3. I am the light of the ____________. (John 8:12)
4. The Lord God will be their ____________. (Revelation 22:5)
5. Walk as ____________ of light. (Ephesians 5:8)
6. You may become ________________ of light. (John 12:36)
7. Seeing the light of the _______. (2 Corinthians 4:4)

Q. What did Jesus say at the Last Supper after "One of you shall betray me"?

A. "Separate checks, please!"

9. One who does ________________ hates light. (John 3:20)

SHORT ANSWER

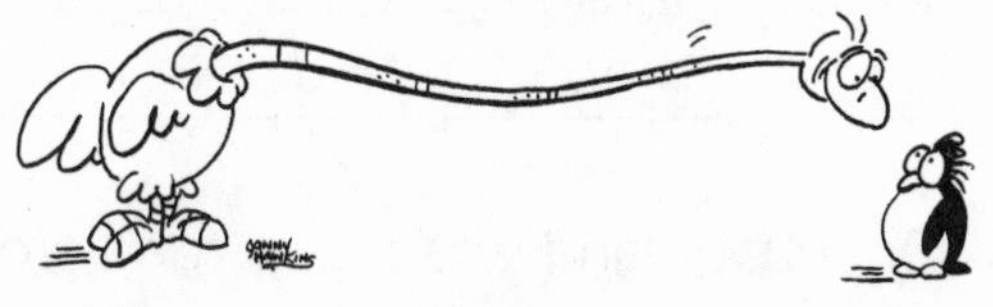

1. What was an alternate name given to the country of the Gergesenes? ________________

2. What place is said to have been a Sabbath day's journey from Jerusalem? ________________

3. Where did the Apostle dwell of whom our Lord stated that he was "an Israelite indeed, in whom is no guile"? ________________

4. Our Savior told his disciples to "shake the dust off" their feet against those cities who refused to receive them. Where did they do this? ________________

____

Q. What else did Jesus say at the Last Supper?

A. "Everyone who wants to be in the picture get on this side of the table."

5. In what town did our Lord spend his last Sabbath?

______

6. What mountain was Christ's abode by night?

______

7. On what island was a ship run aground for safety?

______

8. Where did the Apostles hold their first missionary meeting? ______

9. At what place was St. Paul stoned? ______

10. At what place was Elymas struck blind? ______

11. What city was exalted to heaven yet brought to destruction? ______

12. Where and of whom was it said, "they have turned the world upside down?" ______

13. What was the ruling nation of the Mediterranean world in the time of Christ? ______

14. What city was popularly supposed to produce nothing good? ______

15. Where was an altar erected "to the unknown God"?

______

BIBLE JEOPARDY

$100	$200	$300	$400	DAILY DOUBLE	$500	$600	$700	$800	$900

Here are the answers. Do you know the questions?

1. "He waited for the city which has foundations, whose builder and maker is God."
2. He was able to say, "I have fought a good fight, I have finished the race, I have kept the faith."
3. Christ compared Himself to this part of a sheepfold.
4. He said, "the effectual fervent prayer of a righteous man avails much."
5. He was the cousin of Jesus and his forerunner.

MATCHING

Match those whom Jesus blessed with the blessing they received. Some answers may be used more than once.

1. The poor in spirit	a. Shall inherit the earth
2. Those who mourn	b. Shall see God
3. The meek	c. Theirs is the kingdom of heaven
4. The schizophrenic	d. Shall be comforted

5. Those who hunger and thirst for righteousness	e. Shall have their own talk show
6. The merciful	f. Shall obtain mercy
7. The pure in heart	g. Shall be blessed again and again
8. The peacemakers	h. Shall be called sons of God
9. Those who are persecuted for righteousness' sake	i. Shall be filled
10. The weak in mind	

WORD FIND

Find the names of these book of the New Testament listed below in the puzzle.

R S N A I S E H P E J J S
S O A S W K R A M O A N C
M N M C V W Y L H M A G O
A D A A T I N N E I Y A L
T D W I N S N S N U H L O
T O F R H S J O G M T A S
H N P T V T L U B S O T S
E U O E S A N T D O M I I
W T K U S Q E I R E I A A
Z U T S Y H E R R E T N N
L I E Q A T Q K L O T S S
T H N O M E L I H P C E U
T P H I L I P P I A N S P

Acts	James	Mark	Romans
Colossians	John	Matthew	Thessalonians
Corinthians	Jude	Philemon	Timothy
Ephesians	Luke	Philippians	Titus

ENIGMA NO. 1

1. From where did Israel, precious metal bring?
2. Of what sweet tree did ancient prophets sing?
3. A holy seer who wondrous visions saw.
4. Whose children did obey their father's law?
5. What wicked man did take his brother's life?
6. Who took a city to obtain a wife?
7. Seven of this name are found in holy writ.
8. The land that Israel once in haste did quit.
9. Who uttered forth a deep and bitter cry?
10. Whose son was sent, the Promised Land to spy?
11. What aged saint with deepest grief oppressed, Saw not that all was ordered for the best?
12. Who, when on earth, his sufferings meekly bore, Then, led by angels, up to heaven did soar?
13. Who, with a stone, did once a conqueror slay?
14. Who sent his daughters from their home away?
15. What merchant city once was rich and great, But through its sins was brought to low estate?

16. What man, of peace did falsely prophesy,
And surely offended the Lord, and lo, would die?

17. The mount from where the blessing did proceed.

18. Who helped the prophets in their greatest need?

19. The bird that sat on Babel's ruined towers.

20. A youth who served his God with all his powers.

In the initials of these names combined,
The Lord's command you will surely find;
Which if we humbly from our hearts obey,
Will make us victors in the heavenly way.

QUOTEFALL

ANSWERS
p. 390

Solve the puzzle by moving the letters to form words. The letters can only be moved to another place in the same column. Black boxes indicate the spaces between words. Each word begins in the left side of the box.

A		S			A				Y		
H	R	E	T		O	R	L		Y	N	U
R	A	C	A	F	E	O	R	P	E	O	C
C	I	M	S	R	F	L	U	H	O	O	U
				■				■			
	■					■					■
			■				■			■	
				■				■			

SHORT ANSWER

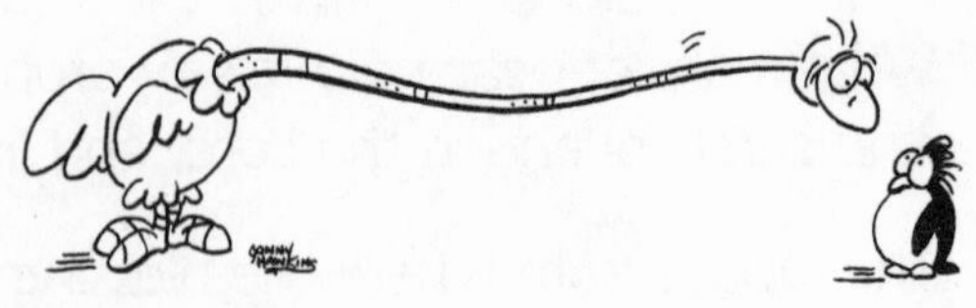

1. Who built the first city? ________________

2. Who was the first sacred historian? ________________

3. Who was the first judge? ________________

4. Who was the first pilgrim? ________________

HOW ABOUT THAT!

"I believe the Bible is the best gift God has ever given to men. All the good from the Savior of the world is communicated to us through this Book."

—President Abraham Lincoln

5. Who was the first shepherd mentioned in the Scriptures? ________________

6. Who told the first lie as recorded in the Scriptures?

____

7. Who was the first Jewish high priest? ________________

8. Who was the first gardener? ________________

9. Who first wore the bridal veil? ________________

10. Who was the first machinist in brass and iron?

____

BIBLE CHARACTER QUIZ

Bible Character 1

I am a flourishing church of Asia Minor. The first letter of each of the proper names described below will give you my name.

1. A Christian householder
2. A kinsman of St. Paul
3. One of the divisions of the Holy Land mentioned in the New Testament

Q. Which area of Palestine was especially wealthy?

A. The area around the Jordan: the banks were always overflowing.

4. A place where St. Paul was in peril from his own countrymen

5. An eloquent man, and one mighty in the Scriptures

6. A city from which St. Paul narrowly escaped with his life

7. The first fruits of Achaia

8. One of the apostles

9. A comforter and helper of St. Paul

10. A political sect among the Jews

11. A division of the Roman army

12. A New Testament prophet

Bible Character 2

I am a noted teacher of Jewish law, whose reasoning had great weight with the council at Jerusalem.

The first letter of each of the proper names described below will give you my name:

1. The portion of Palestine that was the birthplace of many of the apostles.
2. An aged widow remarkable for a life of fasting and prayer.
3. A disciple of Cyprus, with whom Paul lodged during his last visit to Jerusalem.
4. The name of one whose sudden death brought great fear on all the church.
5. The only companion of St. Paul during his last imprisonment at Rome.
6. The city in Asia Minor from whence the Jews came who stoned Paul.
7. The village where our Savior spent the first evening after his resurrection.

Q. What pastry cook is mentioned in the Bible?

A. Paul—he went to Philippi (fill a pie).

8. A city where the apostle Peter ministered to the saints.

FILL IN THE BLANKS

1. "And she will bring forth a Son, and you shall call His name Jesus, for ______________________ ______________________."

2. "But He [Jesus] answered and said, 'It is written, "Man shall not live by bread alone, but __________ ______________________."'"

3. "Then Jesus said to him, '______________________ ______________________ For it is written, "You shall worship the Lord your God, and Him only you shall serve."'"

4. "Then He said to them, 'Follow Me, and I will make you ______________________.'"

5. "Read my lips, ______________________ ______________________."

6. "Blessed are you when they revile and persecute you, and say all kinds of evil against you falsely for My sake. Rejoice and be exceedingly glad, for ______________________________, for so they persecuted the prophets who were before you."

7. "Let your ______________________________, that they may see your good works and glorify your Father in heaven."

8. "But I say to you, ______________________________, bless those who curse you, do good to those who hate you, and pray for those who spitefully use you and persecute you . . ."

9. "But seek first ______________________ and His righteousness, and all these things shall be added to you."

10. "Not everyone who says to Me, 'Lord, Lord,' shall enter the kingdom of heaven, but he who ______ ______________________."

11. "Heal the sick, cleanse the lepers, raise the dead, cast out demons. ______________________, freely give."

12. "Take My yoke upon you and learn from Me, for I am gentle and lowly in heart, and you will ______ ______________. For My yoke is easy and My burden is light."

13. "Who let the ______________?"

14. "Assuredly, I say to you, unless you are converted and ______________________, you will by no means enter the kingdom of heaven."

15. "But Jesus said, 'Let the little children come to Me, and do not forbid them; for ______________.'"

16. "For where two or three are gathered together in My name, ____ ______________________________."

HOW ABOUT THAT!

The term "Devil's Advocate" comes from the Roman Catholic church. When deciding if someone should become a saint, a devil's advocate is always appointed to explore an alternative view.

17. "His lord said to him, '______________________________ ______________________________; you were faithful over a few things, I will make you ruler over many things. Enter into the joy of your lord.'"

18. "And the King will answer and say to them, 'Assuredly, I say to you, inasmuch as you ______________, you did it to Me.'"

19. "Go therefore and make disciples of all the nations, baptizing them in the name of the Father and of the Son and of the Holy Spirit, teaching them to observe

all things that I have commanded you; and lo, ____________________.''

20. ''There are three kinds of people in this world, ____________________________________.''

CRAZY QUOTATIONS

ANSWERS p. 393

Translate this crazy quote into the correct verse.

1. ''Glory to God in the highest,
   And on earth peach, good humor toward
   men!''

2. ''Give, and it will be given to you: good measles, pressed down, shaken to heaven, and running wild will it be put into your bonus. For with the same meter that you utter, it will be measured back to you.''

Q. Who was the smallest man in the Bible?

A. Peter—because he slept on his watch.

3. "Then He said to them all, 'If anyone desires to come after Me, let him defy himself, and take up his cross duly, and fellowship with Me.'"

4. "But He said, 'Merely that, blessed are those who plant the word of God and those who reap it!'"

5. "Do not fear, little children, for it is your Father's good present to give you the kingfish."

6. "For whoever exhibits himself will be humdrum, and he who humdrums himself will be exhibited."

7. "He who is faithless in what is least is faithless also in muck; and he who is useless in what is least is useless also in mire."

ANSWERS TO: GETTING THE QUOTES: NEW TESTAMENT

MULTIPLE CHOICE

#	ANSWER	REFERENCE
1.	c.	Mark 7:37
2.	d.	Matthew 9:36–38
3.	d.	Acts 11:23
4.	a.	Romans 12:1
5.	c.	1 Corinthians 4:2
6.	d.	Luke 9:26
7.	b.	John 9:5
8.	c.	1 Corinthians 5:6
9.	c.	Luke 9:49, 50
10.	d.	Mark 9:29

FILL IN THE BLANKS

#	ANSWER	REFERENCE
1.	and take up his cross daily, and follow Me.	Luke 9:23
2.	and not to please ourselves.	Romans 15:1
3.	shall be saved.	Romans 10:13

FILL IN THE BLANKS—cont'd

#	ANSWER	REFERENCE
4.	Apollos, or Cephas, or the world, or life or death, or things present or things to come—all are yours. And you are Christ's, and Christ is God's.	1 Corinthians 3:21–23
5.	He will draw near to you.	James 4:8
6.	the spirit gives life.	2 Corinthians 3:6
7.	yesterday, and to-day, and forever.	Hebrews 13:8
8.	his life will lose it; his life for My sake, the same	Luke 9:24
9.	There is therefore now no condemnation to those who are in Christ Jesus	Romans 8:1
10.	separate us from the love of Christ?	Romans 8:35
11.	is Christ, and to die is gain.	Philippians 1:21
12.	word, in conduct, in love, in spirit, in faith, in purity.	1 Timothy 4:12
13.	but also for the interests of others.	Philippians 2:4
14.	work out your own salvation with fear and trembling.	Philippians 2:12

#	ANSWER	REFERENCE
15.	the love of the Father is not in him.	1 John 2:15

BIBLE MATH

#	ANSWER				
1.	Commandments + 1	=	11	=	K
	Stones picked up by David + 4	=	9	=	I
	Deacons chosen in Acts 6 X 2	=	14	=	N
	Kings of the Amorites + 2	=	7	=	G
	Lazarus' sisters X 2	=	4	=	D
	Job's friends X 5	=	15	=	O
	Abraham's angelic visitors + 10	=	13	=	M
2.	Spies sent into Canaan – 5	=	7	=	G
	Old Testament books ÷ 2	=	15	=	O
	Abijah's wives – 10	=	4	=	D
3.	Jesus' days in the desert – 17	=	23	=	W
	New Testament books ÷ 3	=	9	=	I
	Silver shekels paid for Joseph	=	20	=	T
	Leaders of men in Micah 5	=	8	=	H
	Jonah's days inside the whale X 3	=	9	=	I
	Jesse's sons + 6	=	14	=	N

BIBLE MATH—cont'd

#	ANSWER				
4.	Elders in Revelation + 1	=	25	=	Y
	Lepers healed by Jesus + 5	=	15	=	O
	Chapters in Judges	=	21	=	U

The K I N G D O M of G O D

is W I T H I N Y O U.

TRUE OR FALSE?

#	ANSWER	REFERENCE
1.	False; James.	James 2:20.
2.	False; God and mammon.	Matthew 6:24
3.	True.	James 3:5
4.	False; The parable speaks of the fault-finder who ignores a plank in his own eye while he seeks to remove a speck from his brother's eye. Its meaning is clean up your own act before you criticize somebody else's behavior.	Matthew 7:1–5
5.	True.	Romans 8:28

#	ANSWER	REFERENCE
6.	False; "For no other foundation can anyone lay than that which is laid, which is Jesus Christ."	1 Corinthians 3:11
7.	False; "You ask and do not receive, because you ask amiss, that you may spend it on your pleasures."	James 4:3
8.	False; To the church at Philadelphia.	Revelation 3:7, 8
9.	True.	Luke 7:14
10.	False; In unbelieving Nazareth.	Mark 6:1–6

CROSSWORD PUZZLE

SHORT ANSWER

#	ANSWER	REFERENCE
1.	The country of the Gadarenes	Matthew 8:28; Mark 5:1
2.	Mount Olivet	Acts 1:12
3.	Cana in Galilee	John 1:47
4.	At Antioch in Pisidia	Acts 13:14
5.	Bethany	Matthew 26:6; Mark 14:3; John 12:1
6.	Mount of Olives	Luke 21:37; John 8:1
7.	Malta	Acts 27 and 28
8.	Antioch	Acts 14:26
9.	Lystra	Acts 14:19
10.	Paphos in Cyprus	Acts 13:6
11.	Capernaum	Matthew 11:23
12.	At Thessalonica, of the disciples	Acts 17:1–6
13.	Rome	Luke 2:1
14.	Nazareth	John 1:46
15.	Athens	Acts 17:22

BIBLE JEOPARDY

#	ANSWER	
1.	Who is Abraham, the sojourner?	Hebrews 11:10
2.	Who is Paul?	2 Timothy 4:7
3.	What is a door?	John 10:1–9
4.	Who is James?	James 5:16
5.	Who was John the Baptist?	Mark 1:1–14

MATCHING

#	ANSWER	REFERENCE
1.	c.	Matthew 5:3
2.	d.	Matthew 5:4
3.	a.	Matthew 5:5
4.	g.	
5.	i.	Matthew 5:6
6.	f.	Matthew 5:7
7.	b.	Matthew 5:8
8.	h.	Matthew 5:9
9.	c.	Matthew 5:10
10.	e.	Shall have their own talk show

WORD FIND

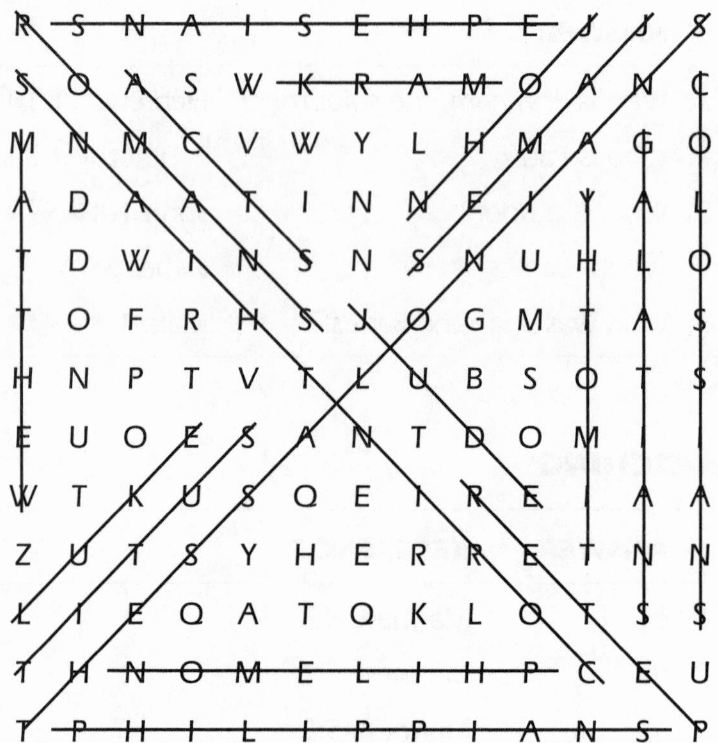

ENIGMA NO. 1

# ANSWER	REFERENCE
"OVERCOME EVIL WITH GOOD."	Romans 12:21
1. **O**-phir	2 Chronicles 8:18
2. **V**-ine	Isaiah 5:1

#	ANSWER	REFERENCE
3.	**E**-zekiel	Ezekiel 1:1
4.	**R**-echabites	Jeremiah 35
5.	**C**-ain	Genesis 4:8
6.	**O**-thniel	Judges 1:12, 13
7.	**M**-ary	Exodus 10:20; 1 Chronicles 4:17
8.	**E**-gypt.	Exodus 20:33
9.	**E**-sau.	Genesis 27:34
10.	**V**-ophsis	Numbers 13:14
11.	**I**-srael	Genesis 42:30.
12.	**L**-azarus	Luke 16:20.
13.	**W**-omen of Thebez	Judges 9:50.
14.	**I**-bzan	Judges 12:8, 9.
15.	**T**-yre.	Ezekiel 27:28.
16.	**H**-ananiah	Daniel. 1:7.
17.	**G**-erizim	Deuteronomy 11:29.
18.	**O**-badiah.	1 Kings 13:4.
19.	**O**-wl	Isaiah 13:19.
20.	**D**-aniel	Ezekiel 14:14; Daniel 14:14.

Q. How do we know Peter was a rich fisherman?

A. By his net income.

QUOTEFALL

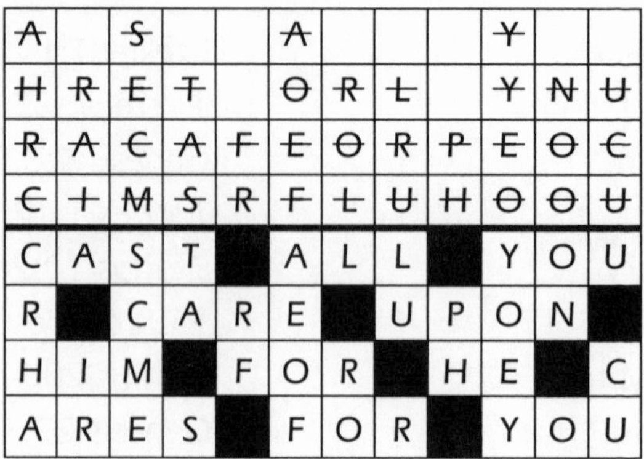

SHORT ANSWER

#	ANSWER	REFERENCE
1.	Cain; The city of Enoch	Genesis 4:17
2.	Moses	Numbers 1:1
3.	Moses	Exodus 18:13
4.	Abram	Genesis 12:1, 6
5.	Abel	Genesis 4:4
6.	Cain	Genesis 4:8
7.	Aaron	Exodus 28:1
8.	Adam	Genesis 2:15
9.	Rebekah	Genesis 24:64, 65
10.	Tubal-Cain	Genesis 4:22

BIBLE CHARACTER QUIZ

Bible Character 1—PHILADELPHIA

#	ANSWER	REFERENCE
Revelation 1:11		
1.	**P**-hilemon	Philemon 1:2
2.	**H**-erodion	Romans 16:11
3.	**I**-turaea	Luke 3:1
4.	**L**-ystra	Acts 14:19
5.	**A**-pollos	Acts 18:24
6.	**D**-amascus	2 Corinthians 11:32, 33
7.	**E**-penetus	Romans 16:5
8.	**L**-ebbaeus	Matthew 10:3
9.	**P**-hebe	Romans 16:1. 2
10.	**H**-erodians	Matthew 22:16
11.	**I**-talian Band	Acts 10:1
12.	**A**-gabus	Acts 21:10

Bible Character 2—GAMALIEL

#	ANSWER	REFERENCE
Acts 5:34		
1.	**G**-alilee	Acts 2:7
2.	**A**-nna	Luke 2:36
3.	**M**-nason	Acts 21:16

BIBLE CHARACTER QUIZ—cont'd

#	ANSWER	REFERENCE
4.	**A**-nanias	Acts 5:5
5.	**L**-uke	2 Timothy 4:11
6.	**I**-conium	Acts 14:19
7.	**E**-mmaus	Luke 24:3
8.	**L**-ydda	Acts 9:32

FILL IN THE BLANKS

#	ANSWER	REFERENCE
1.	"for He will save His people from their sins"	Matthew 1:21
2.	"by every word that proceeds from the mouth of God"	Matthew 4:4
3.	"Away with you, Satan!"	Matthew 4:10
4.	"fishers of men"	Matthew 4:19
5.	"No new taxes"	
6.	"great is your reward in heaven"	Matthew 5:11–12
7.	"light so shine before men"	Matthew 5:16

#	ANSWER	REFERENCE
8.	"love your enemies"	Matthew 5:44
9.	"the kingdom of God"	Matthew 6:33
10.	"does the will of My Father in heaven"	Matthew 7:21
11.	"Freely you have received"	Matthew 10:8
12.	"find rest for your souls"	Matthew 11:29–30
13.	"dogs out, who, who, who?"	
14.	"become as little children"	Matthew 18:3
15.	"of such is the kingdom of heaven"	Matthew 19:14
16.	"I am there in the midst of them"	Matthew 18:20
17.	"Well done, good and faithful servant"	Matthew 25:21
18.	"did it to one of the least of these My brethren"	Matthew 25:40
19.	"I am with you always, even to the end of the age"	Matthew 28:19–20
20.	"Those who can count, and those who can't"	

CRAZY QUOTATIONS

#	ANSWER	REFERENCE
1.	"Glory to God in the highest, and on earth peace, goodwill toward men!"	Luke 2:14
2.	"Give, and it will be given to you: good measure, pressed down, shaken together, and running over will be put into your bosom. For with the same measure that you use, it will be measured back to you."	Luke 6:38
3.	"Then He said to them all, 'If anyone desires to come after Me, let him deny himself, and take up his cross daily, and follow Me.'"	Luke 9:23
4.	"But He said, 'More than that, blessed are those who hear the word of God and keep it!'"	Luke 11:28
5.	"Do not fear, little flock, for it is your Father's good pleasure to give you the kingdom."	Luke 12:32
6.	"For whoever exalts himself will be humbled, and he who humbles himself will be exalted."	Luke 14:11

#	ANSWER	REFERENCE
7.	"He who is faithful in what is least is faithful also in much; and he who is unjust in what is least is unjust also in much."	Luke 16:10

ABOUT THE AUTHOR

Rev. Lowell (Lowell D. Streiker) is an inspirational humorist, speaker, and author whose personal experience ranges from appearing on the Oprah Winfrey Show to advising the White House. In recent years, he has spoken to audiences of up to 5000 in the United States, Norway, Finland, Russia, Poland and Hungary. His book, *An Encyclopedia of Humor,* is a current best seller. His most recent humor book is *Nelson's Big Book of Laughter.*

His home is at Lone Pine Ranch, 3309 El Camino Drive, Cottonwood, CA 96022. Phone (530) 347-1948, Fax: (530) 347-5617, email: revlowell@earthlink.net.

Rev. Lowell is an ordained minister in the United Church of Christ and holds a Ph.D. in religion from Princeton University.

Math puzzles used throughout this book are the contribution of Carrie L. Clickhard of CL Enterprises and Word Works.

OTHER TITLES IN THE SERIES

- *Nelson's Amazing Bible Trivia: Book One,* Brad Densmore
  Think the Bible is boring? Think again! With over 5,000 Bible questions and answers, top ten lists, and stumpers, this book will appeal to everyone. This unique Bible Trivia book holds a unique collection of curious facts, unusual statistics, and fascinating questions from the Bible. From Genesis to Revelation, there are questions and answers from every book in the Bible that is fun for the whole family!

- *Nelson's Amazing Bible Trivia: Book Two*
  Laugh and learn more about the Bible! Book Two of Bible Trivia is a hilarious sequel to Book One. This book captures the humor and enigma of the first work and issues new puzzles, multiple choice, matching, fill-in-the-blank, and much more. Also, it includes curious facts, unusual and fascinating lists that are great for parties, Sunday morning services, youth groups, and classes. Enjoy learning about the scriptures in a whole new way!